• **Batholc**

WALK THE
NEW FOREST
by Jill Brown and David Skelhon

Bartholomew

A Division of HarperCollins*Publishers*

A Bartholomew Walk Guide
Published by Bartholomew
HarperCollins*Publishers*
77-85 Fulham Palace Road
London W6 8JB

First published 1988
This revised edition 1994.

© Bartholomew 1994

Printed in Great Britain by Bartholomew.
The Edinburgh Press Ltd.

ISBN 0 7028 2543 3
88/2/45   G/J6501

Britain's landscape is changing all the time. While every care has
been taken in the preparation of this guide, Bartholomew and
Curtis Garratt Limited accept no responsibility whatsoever for any
loss, damage, injury or inconvenience sustained or caused as a
result of using this guide.

CONTENTS

KEY MAP FOR THE WALKS

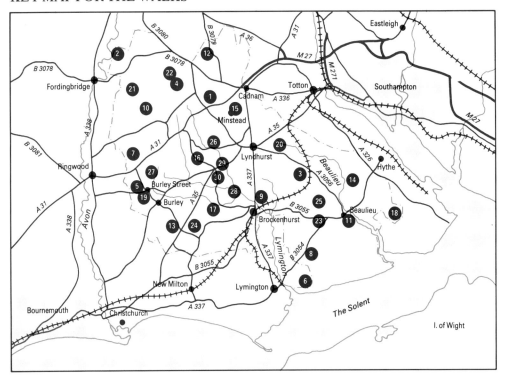

KEY TO SCALE AND MAP SYMBOLS

SCALE 1 : 63 360

SCALE 1 : 25 000

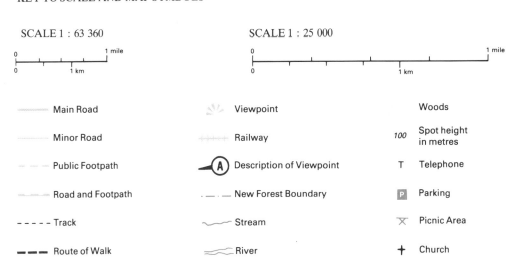

Main Road	Viewpoint	Woods
Minor Road	Railway	*100* Spot height in metres
Public Footpath	(A) Description of Viewpoint	T Telephone
Road and Footpath	New Forest Boundary	P Parking
Track	Stream	Picnic Area
Route of Walk	River	+ Church

1 THE WALKER'S FOREST

The New Forest is the largest area of lowland heath in Britain and, ecologically, probably the most important in Europe. Its combination of heathland, valley mire and ancient pasture woodland occur nowhere else in such combination or on such a scale. The unique history of land management has meant they are relatively undisturbed and rich in species and in recognition of all this the whole of the Forest is a designated Site of Special Scientific Interest with the status of a national nature reserve. It lies in south-west Hampshire between the highly industrialised Southampton Water to the east and the tranquil Avon to the west. The Hampshire chalklands lay close to its northern limits and, from the highest point of 422 feet (129 m), its gentle gravel and sand ridges, valleys and plains slip quietly into the Solent some 17 miles (27 km) to the south.

Almost a quarter of its 150 or so square miles (260 sq km) are covered with silvicultural inclosures - mainly coniferous. Another quarter of the land is occupied by farms and villages. The remaining half is a mixture of open woodland valley mires, heather- and gorse-clad heathland, and grassy forest lawns.

Lazy streams dissect the Forest, bringing brown, iron-stained water from the many mires to the Solent or to the River Avon. Ponds, usually artificial, also stud the heath.

Three-quarters of the land within the Forest boundary (or perambulation, as it is known) is owned by the Crown, and managed by the Forestry Commission and the Verderers. The latter are representatives both of the commoners, who turn out their ponies, cattle, and pigs on to the Forest, and also of other parties with an interest in the Forest's welfare.

The public is permitted access on foot or horseback on to Crown land and is free to wander at will through heath and Forest - a rare privilege in England today. Much of the private land is also crossed by public rights of way.

The Forestry Commission has provided for walkers numerous car parks in all corners of the Forest, and there are also seven official campsites where they may stay. Even so, the Forest is under great pressure from the 8 million visitors who, each year seek its peace and tranquillity. It is rather surprising, therefore, that, in the peak season when the villages are bursting with people and the roads roaring with traffic, the walker may spend hours roaming the more remote Forest with only the animals for company.

The Forest's attraction is more subtle than that of the wilder, upland areas of

Britain. The desire to cover distance takes second place to leisurely observation and contemplation. Even the rivers dawdle, taking time to rest in deep, sunlit pools.

The walkers will often find themselves sharing the landscape with other creatures. Most obvious are the commoners' ponies and cattle, ambling along contentedly as they graze their way through the Forest. The deer are more elusive and can often be seen on the remoter walks if you are not seen or heard by them first!

All around, is the wildlife of the countryside. Green woodpeckers alight from the heath on hearing your approach, sounding their distinctive laughing cry and bobbing off into the distance. Above the summer gorse and heather, the air is filled with the hum of bees and the twitter of meadow pipits, while appropriately named stonechats 'chink' noisily as they nervously watch you pass by.

On the heath, a dry, sandy trail may suddenly give way to a muddy mire, white with the tufts of cotton grass and teeming with a different collection of wildlife. At a welcome pool, 100 or so ponies and cattle may congregate under a blazing sun to cool off and quench their thirsts.

There is also, of course, the wonder of some of the most remarkable woodland in Europe, with its majestic oaks and beech. Seemingly neglected, it probably resembles the ancient wildwood in structure and atmosphere and provides one of the richest wildlife habitats in Britain. After 300 years or more, many of the trees are crumbling and being returned to the soil by a micro-world of colourful insects and fungi.

The sometimes strange and evocative place names will interest the walker, too - Mark Ash, Ragged Boys Hill, Bushey Bratley, and Smugglers Way, to name but a few. These are waymarks on a journey back in time. Indeed, if we were to travel back 900 years to the reign of William the Conqueror, we would find the Forest landscape much as it is today, remaining, thanks to almost a millennium of Forest law - a unique medieval island in a sea of change.

2 CLOTHING AND EQUIPMENT

We are fortunate that the New Forest has a relatively kind climate which usually allows the walker to travel light during the summer months.

Lightweight leather boots worn over thick socks are the ideal footwear for Forest trails. For particularly wet weather, wellingtons are useful for short walks because they ensure dry feet when walking through wet grass and boggy areas. In periods of unsettled summer weather and certainly throughout the winter, it is advisable to carry a lightweight waterproof. These also give protection from chilling winds when walking on exposed heaths. Waterproof overtrousers are also useful, not only in the rain but also when walking through dew-laden bracken which can quickly leave you soaked from the waist down.

For the longer excursions, it is a good idea to carry some energy-giving fruit or chocolate and something to drink. You may be out for three or four hours and, in the sparsely populated Forest, you are unlikely to pass a café or a pub.

A pair of binoculars is particularly useful and adds a new dimension to any walk. The New Forest is rich in bird and animal life and, to the uninitiated with average eyesight, every small bird may look like a sparrow!

diverse and colourful nature of our native species. Deer, too, may be stalked undisturbed with their aid. For walkers, a pair of 8x30s are small and light yet powerful enough for most purposes.

A 1:25 000 map and compass are useful aids to route finding when used in conjunction with this book.

Finally, all these items are best carried in a lightweight rucksack. Nothing large or heavy is required for daywalking and for comfort choose a design with wide, padded shoulderstraps.

3 MAP READING

The New Forest lacks natural and artificial landmarks that would make route-finding easier. Unlike on the moors and mountains of upland Britain, however, being lost in the New Forest is often more inconvenient than hazardous.

Nevertheless, do beware of being caught out in woodland late in the day, for light fades more quickly among the trees than on the heath – it is best to be back at the car before dusk.

With the aid of a 1:25 000 map and a compass (the 'Silva' type is ideal and readily obtainable) the walker should rarely find himself/herself completely lost, even in the deepest Forest. Do not be discouraged by the thought of using a compass, for navigation is a skill that is easily learnt. In any case, the techniques needed in this terrain are very simple and basic. The main problem is the lack of identifiable landmarks but, if you follow your route from the very beginning and make frequent checks, there will be few difficulties.

To confirm your position, orientate the map with the compass so that the grid of the map lies in line with the needle of the compass, which should point to the top of the map. You should be able to verify any feature on the ground with those on the map – a stream, a cottage, a junction, and so on. Doing this frequently will mean that, if any error has occurred, your steps can quickly be retraced before a lot of unexpected ground has been covered.

A word of warning, though, maps quickly become outdated, and indicated features may not agree with those found in the field. In particular, boundary fences are removed when inclosures are thrown open, whole areas of plantation may be felled, forest trails fall out of use and become overgrown, while others are created for various reasons.

In the New Forest expect to cover about 2 to 2½ miles per hour (3¼–4 km/h) allowing for short stops along the way, although this will obviously vary from person to person. If you are unsure of your position and have been using a compass, you will know roughly where you have been heading. Study the map and proceed along a compass bearing that is most likely to lead to a road.

All this may sound like a little too much hard work on what should be a relaxing walk, but these skills soon become second nature and enable the walker to penetrate the remoter parts of the Forest with confidence.

4 THE COUNTRY CODE

The country code can be summed up with the well-known adage 'leave only footprints, take only photographs'. All it takes is a little care and thought. Do not, for instance, drop litter – fluorescent orange peel, crushed drink cans, and brightly coloured chocolate wrappers do not blend well with the environment!

Shut all gates behind you and use the proper stiles to cross fences and hedges where provided. On narrow paths, walk in single file to avoid erosion.

Take care not to disturb wildlife and remember that the Wildlife and Countryside Act of 1981 gives strong protection to many wild creatures. In particular, keep dogs under close control – they can cause considerable disturbance to wildlife. Do not be tempted to rescue a young bird or animal that appears to have been abandoned – its parents are anxiously waiting for you to disappear so they can perform their own rescue!

Some plants have special protection and must not be picked intentionally. The safest approach is to pick none at all – in any case, the flowers are there for all to enjoy.

During dry weather the Forest is a tinder box. Open fires or carelessly discarded cigarette ends can produce catastrophic results.

Finally, do not feed the ponies because this makes them associate food with people and attracts them to the roads, where they may cause accidents.

The Country Code is based on common sense. You will offend no-one if you leave the countryside as you found it.

5   PUBLIC ACCESS TO THE NEW FOREST

Only a few well-signposted public footpaths and bridleways across private land are included in the walks in this book, so only the essential points regarding public rights of way are given here.

Public footpaths are intended for use by walkers only, but public bridleways can be used for passage on foot, bicycle, or horseback. Although it may often prove impractical, pushchairs, prams, wheelchairs and invalid carriages may be used on either. Cycling is only permitted on bridleways and "forest roads", the latter marked on the 1:25 000 maps as black double pecked lines.

It is up to the walker to ensure that he or she keeps to the designated path, for if he/she wanders away from it - either deliberately or unintentionally - he/she may be trespassing. Walkers may linger to admire the view or to eat lunch but must not obstruct a right of way.

The walker has the right to remove an obstruction from a right of way just to get past, but cannot go on to a public right of way with prior knowledge of an obstruction and the intention to remove it. Growing crops are the most common obstruction. You are entitled to walk through them even if this means some damage is unavoidable. Often this is unpleasant and, with some mature crops, virtually impossible. In these circumstances, you may go around the crop, but it is advisable to stay within the field boundary to avoid trespassing on someone else's land.

Once on Crown land, under the control of the Forestry Commission, the walker may wander where he/she pleases. Keep to well-made paths wherever possible, however, to avoid unnecessary disturbance to wildlife.

6 GEOLOGY

The single most important factor in shaping

the New Forest as we know it today is the underlying rocks – mainly soft sands, clays, and gravels which produce poor, acid soils. To understand the surrounding landscape and its origins, we need to travel back over 100 million years to a time when England and the near continent were submerged beneath a clear, warm sea. The skeletons of plankton and marine creatures, rich in calcium carbonate, sank to the bottom of the sea and, over millions of years, accumulated and consolidated to form chalk rock thousands of feet thick. Eventually this chalk, covering much of England, was uplifted and subjected to the erosive agents of sun, wind, and rain.

Some 65 million years ago, the land sank and the south of England became a coastal region. Rivers poured into the sea, dumping sands, silts, and clays over this area as the land repeatedly rose and fell for millions of years. It is these deposits that, in many places, lie directly beneath the Forest's soils.

This period of deposition ended about 30 million years ago when cataclysmic earth movements, known as the 'Alpine Storm', threw up the great mountain ranges of Europe. Great stresses were felt in Britain, too, and the chalk and sediments beneath the New Forest buckled into a shallow basin or syncline. Today, after another 30 million years of erosion, the rim of this basin is exposed as the Hampshire and Dorset chalklands to the north and west and the spine of the Isle of Wight to the south. The sediments of the New Forest lying within this basin tilt downwards by about 2 degrees towards the Solent and have been eroded so that the oldest rocks are exposed in the north and the youngest in the south.

The fertility of the Forest soils depends largely on the deposition conditions of the underlying sediments. The oldest and poorest sands, which dominate the northern Forest, were probably laid down as coastal sandbars and spits, while the more fertile loams, clays, and marls of the south originate from shallow seas and mudflats similar to those found in estuaries today.

The main modification, other than erosion, has been the deposition of thin layers of gravel and brickearth (a mixture of sand, silt, and clay) that has occurred during the glaciations of the Ice Ages. These gravels and brickearths cap most of the ridges and fill the occasional valley. They were most probably deposited by the River Solent over the last 2 million years while it cut a progressively more south-easterly course to its present position.

7 PLANTS AND ANIMALS OF THE NEW FOREST

The living world of today's Forest results from the complex interactions of people and their domestic animals with the rest of nature. For instance, since the Bronze Age, people have encouraged their animals to graze and browse the Forest and, as a consequence, palatable saplings, such as the once-common lime and hazel, became increasingly scarce and are now eliminated from the Forest. This has left open pasture woodlands predominantly of oak and beech with an understorey of holly. Scots pine was extinct in southern England until it was re-introduced in the eighteenth century. It is now common, especially on the heathland which it is rapidly colonizing.

Beech has a very dense canopy which excludes a lot of light and prevents the growth of vegetation on the forest floor. But, in the lighter, oak-dominated woods, the plant life at ground level is much more prolific, with plants, such as the wood anemone, wood sorrel, wood spurge, butcher's-broom, bugle, and enchanter's nightshade. The woodland edges are also the last stronghold in Britain of the beautiful wild gladiolus.

Pedunculate oak is by far the most important tree in the Forest and supports more wildlife than any other British tree. In fact, the ancient woodland is very rich in insect life, mainly because much fallen timber is allowed to decay naturally rather than being sawn up and carted away. The spectacular stag beetle, for instance, depends on decaying timber in its larval stages, and is common in the Forest although it is rare elsewhere in Britain.

Many species of wasp live in the woodland, most notably the large hornet, which nests in holes in old trees, while the woodland edge forms a last refuge for the rare New Forest cicada. It is a peculiar insect, its larvae spending up to seventeen years underground before emerging for a few weeks as an adult.

Many birds of the ancient woodland rely on seeds and on the rich invertebrate life for their existence. Among these there are several species of tits, wrens, thrushes, robins, chaffinches, blackbirds, redstarts, spotted flycatchers, treecreepers, nuthatches, and green, great, and lesser spotted woodpeckers.

The conifer plantations, however, are poor in plants and animals because of the gloomy shade cast by dense planting. The trees do, however, provide homes for goldcrests, firecrests, crossbills, siskins, and redpolls.

Three types of heather are found on the heath – common, bell, and cross-leaved. Gorse and dwarf gorse are also common. In damper areas, there are heath-spotted orchids and insectivorous plants such as the sundew.

A very widespread plant is the low-growing tormentil, with its four yellow petals.

Birds of the heath include stonechats, skylarks, meadow pipits, linnets, and the rare Dartford warbler.

Notable reptiles are the grass snake, the rare smooth snake, and the venomous adder. The scarce sand lizard, the common lizard, and the slowworm (a legless lizard) are also found in the Forest.

The Forest's mires are very important ecologically because they sustain a great variety of plants. They consist of peat enriched with nutrients washed out of the soil in their catchment areas. The streams are usually flanked with alder or willow carr. Bog myrtle – a bushy plant with aromatic leaves – is characteristic of these wetland areas. Other notable plants include bog asphodel, marsh gentian, and bog orchid. Amphibians attracted to these areas are the palmate, smooth, and great crested newt, and the common frog.

Reed buntings are typical birds of the streams and rivers, which are also visited by teal and mallard ducks, herons, and waders such as the snipe, redshank, and curlew during the spring.

Of all the Forest animals, the deer are the most spectacular. Red deer are the largest native species and there are about 150 in the Forest today. Fallow deer were once extinct in the Forest, but it is believed that they were re-introduced by the Normans and now number about 1000. Roe deer are our smallest native species and the most secretive. There are about 250 in the Forest. Japanese sika deer were introduced from the Beaulieu estate early this century and now number around 150. At one time, there may have been 10 000 deer in the Forest but today their numbers are controlled by culling. Other Forest mammals include foxes, badgers, rabbits, grey squirrels, and bats.

Finally, our discussion of Forest animals would be incomplete without mention of the 3000 or so New Forest ponies. This hardy animal probably originates from native ponies but today is in no sense 'wild' because each one has an owner responsible for its welfare. It has evolved to suit the environment and, on occasions, new blood has been introduced to improve the breed. They are very good natured and make excellent children's riding ponies.

8 A BRIEF HISTORY OF THE NEW FOREST

At first sight, people appear to have had little impact on the New Forest – nothing could seem more natural than miles of unfenced heath and rambling woodland. Nevertheless, humans were the architects of the Forest as we see it today; left to its own devices, nature would have given us something very different.

Mankind probably had little impact on the Forest until about 3000 years ago when Bronze Age peoples began clearance for cultivation on a significant scale. Unfortunately, the felling of trees on these poor sandy soils quickly led to a washing away of nutrients and the gradual establishment of heathland. There are more than 200 round barrows dating from this period, most of which have been excavated or vandalized, but they have yielded little besides pottery.

The Iron Age is poorly represented in the Forest but there are defensive settlements at Castle Hill near Burley and others overlooking the Lymington and Beaulieu estuaries. There is little evidence of Roman occupation either. There are remains of potteries, mainly in the Fritham area, however, that date from the third and fourth centuries AD. Not much is known of Saxon times but Domesday records that the settlement patterns we know today were already in existence.

The New Forest was formed by William I some time between the Conquest and his death in 1086, and the actual boundary has changed little since it was extended in 1964. It is unlikely that the Forest was formed solely for the King's pleasure to hunt deer – more likely, its main function was to supply venison and hides for troops.

Its establishment required enforcement of strict Forest laws – possession of bows and arrows was illegal and large dogs had to be 'lamed' so that they were unable to chase the deer. Land that provided cover could not be cleared, and nothing was to interfere with the run of the deer.

Early historians wrote that William I ordered the destruction of villages to establish the Forest, but no evidence of this exists. More likely, it arose from ill feelings of the defeated Saxon chroniclers toward their Norman rulers.

It seems that the population were given the rights to graze their animals in the Forest at certain times of the year and were allowed tax relief in compensation for the harsh Forest laws. These laws were relaxed somewhat in Henry III's Forest charter of 1217 and, eventually, the importance of the Forest as a deer reserve gave way to its potential as a source of timber.

The seventeenth century saw a rapid increase in naval shipbuilding which put great demands on the Forest's resources. Charles II became concerned at the state of New Forest timber production, and nursery plantations were established in the 1670s. Much of the Forest was being coppiced to provide winter fodder for deer, but good building timber was also being removed under this guise so, in 1698, an Act of Parliament made coppicing illegal and this effectively stopped the practice. The Act also required that 2000 acres (800 ha) of oak should be planted immediately, followed by a further 200 acres (80 ha) per year for the next twenty years. Actual planting fell short of this, however, and a report of 1789 revealed that timber production was still taking second place to venison, with little progress made in improving timber resources.

The nineteenth century brought a more professional attitude to forestry and, following an Act of Parliament in 1808, almost 6000 acres (2400 ha) of Forest were inclosed and planted. There then followed the Deer Removal Act in 1851, which unsuccessfully tried to eradicate deer from the Forest. It also authorized the inclosure of a further 10 000 acres (4000 ha) for plantation, with the concession to the commoners that no more than 16 000 acres (6400 ha) of Forest could be inclosed at any one time.

Considerable opposition followed the Act as it became clear that the final aim was disafforestation, with the subsequent inclosure of land and loss of the ancient rights of common. The most important of these rights include the Common of Pasture – the right to graze animals on common land; the Common of Pannage – which allows pigs to forage in autumn for beech mast and acorns; and the Common of Estover – the right to gather firewood from the Forest.

Never before had the Forest been at such risk, and vigorous opposition produced a complete reversal of Parliamentary opinion. This resulted in the 1877 Act which basically prevented any further inclosure. It also had the far-sighted provision that ancient woodlands should be conserved for their aesthetic value.

There has since been a period of relative, but not frictionless, stability between the commoners on the one hand - who depend on their rights for income - and the Crown which requires revenue from timber production. Since 1923, the Crown's interest has been looked after by the Forestry Commission. The Commission is largely responsible for the day-to-day running of the Forest but works jointly with the Verderers.

Since 1949, there have been ten Verderers in all. Five are appointed by the commoners, one is appointed by the Crown, and the other four by interested parties. The Verderers' Court has medieval origins and still sits bimonthly, although its function now is largely administrative.

The Verderers' Agisters carry out the Court's duties, which often involve rounding up the 5000 or so ponies and cattle for marking and rescuing injured animals. The Agisters also have to collect marking fees, which are required of all commoners' animals roaming the Forest.

The post-war years brought a dramatic increase in Forest traffic, especially from tourism, and with it an unacceptable increase in road accidents involving commoners' animals.

The absence of cattle grids meant that Forest cattle and ponies were regular and unwelcome visitors to towns as far away as Christchurch and Salisbury. Many animals were also 'kept' on adjacent commons - although allowed to wander into the forest - so that their owners could avoid marking fees. As a consequence, the New Forest Act of 1964 expanded the boundary to include these commons, and all roads leading from the Forest were either fenced or fitted with cattle grids to prevent stock from wandering.

During the 1960s, pressure from tourism

came to a head; thousands of cars visited the Forest daily during the peak holiday season, and many found their way along tracks deep into its interior, along with caravans and tents. Fortunately, decisive action was taken in the form of car-free areas, authorised car parks, picnic areas, and campsites, saving the Forest from an environmental crisis.

At the same time, extensive felling of deciduous woodlands, and their replacement by conifer plantations, also threatened the Forest on aesthetic and ecological grounds. Public outcry prompted the government to intervene and take action to prevent further destruction of ancient and ornamental woodlands, which were to be 'conserved without regard to timber production objectives'.

Today, a variety of public bodies have a say and responsibility in the planning and management of the Forest resources. Besides the Forestry Commission and the Verderers are the Nature Conservancy Council, the Countryside Commission, the County Council and the District Council. All these are represented on the New Forest Committee, whose task is to look further than the day to day administration at the overall trends affecting the Forest.

Current issues include commercial pressures from industry and mineral exploitation as well as the sheer increase in visitor numbers and traffic. The amount of animal fatalities and the crumbling roads persuaded the authorities to introduce new measures in the last few years including a 40mph speed restriction and physical speed restraint devices on some roads.

With so much concern and involvement, it would seem likely that the unique nature of the Forest can be essentially preserved and its capacity to satisfy the varied demands made on it for timber, grazing, public amenity and, not least, a haven for threatened wildlife, now seems assured into the twenty first century.

9 FURTHER READING

Forestry Commission. 2nd ed. 1987. *Explore the New Forest.* HMSO.

Pasmore, Anthony. 1977. *Verderers of the New Forest.* Pioneer Publications Limited.

Sibley, Patricia and Fletcher, Robin. 1986. *Discovering the New Forest.* Robert Hale.

Sumner, Heywood. 1972. *The New Forest.* Dolphin Press.

Tubbs, Colin R 1986. *The New Forest (A Natural History).* Collins.

THE RUFUS STONE AND LOWER CANTERTON

3 miles (5 km) Easy; some mud

The Rufus Stone stands within earshot of the A31, a continuation of the M27, and the busiest road through the New Forest. Its accessibility and the lure of mystery make it one of the most visited spots in the Forest, although the rather stark monument may be a little disappointing. Not so the surrounding area, which is a pleasant blend of Forest lawn, open woodland, and quiet hamlets.

The walk starts from the Rufus Stone and follows grassy tracks close to the A31 before turning into the tangled depths of Long-beech Inclosure. It emerges at the Sir Walter Tyrell, a welcome stop for refreshments perhaps, before continuing to Lower Canterton where great oaks rise from the forest lawn and stand guard to the depths of Bignell Wood beyond.

A The mystery surrounding the death of William Rufus, the second Norman king of England and son of William the Conqueror, tantalizes like an unfinished Agatha Christie novel.

The three sided cast-iron 'stone' tells us:

> Here stood the oak tree on which an arrow shot by Sir Walter Tyrell at a stag glanced and struck King William II surnamed Rufus on the breast, of which stroke he instantly died on the second day of August anno 1100.
>
> King William II being thus slain was laid on a cart belonging to one Purkess and drawn from hence to Winchester, and buried in the cathedral church of that city.

We know from early historians that William Rufus was a thoroughly nasty character, despised by all his subjects. He was a small, ungainly man with a face redder than his hair, and each eye had a different colour.

His brother Henry and Sir Walter Tyrell were among the hunting party on that fateful August day. All accounts agree that an arrow shot after a stag by Sir Walter glanced off the animal or a tree and struck the king in the chest, killing him instantly. What occurred next seems highly suspicious.

The King's body was carted off to Winchester and buried without ceremony in the cathedral. Henry went to Winchester to demand the Treasury keys and then went on to London, where he was crowned three days later. All this happened amid protestations from William de Breneuil, who was rightfully trying to claim the throne for Henry's elder brother Robert, Duke of Normandy, who was perhaps conveniently out of the country on a crusade.

Meanwhile, Sir Walter had fled to Normandy stopping only, it is said, to have his horse's shoes reversed to confuse pursuers! In the event there were none and Sir Walter later returned to lead a comfortable life in England.

Ironically, it has been suggested that the Rufus Stone is in the wrong place. Canterton Glen was traditionally held to be the spot, and the original stone was placed here by John Lord Delaware in 1745. This was later encased in iron to protect it from vandalism. Recently discovered documentary evidence indicates that Rufus was killed at the southern edge of the Forest near the Solent.

Over

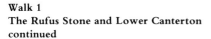

4 *Cross the stream and continue on the path to an open glade. Turn right on to the well-worn path near the end of the glade and follow this to the road by the Sir Walter Tyrell.*

5 *Turn left and follow the road for almost ½ mile (800 m). Turn right down a bridleway near a post box where the road bends left, and follow this to Lower Canterton.*

6 *Turn right and follow the track to Greys Farm, then bear half-left following the line of a small gulley into the trees. Carry stright on into an open area and keep to its right-hand edge as far as the corner.*

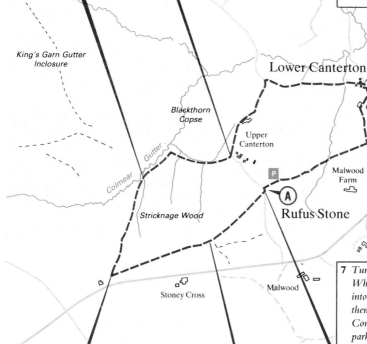

7 *Turn right on to a grassy track. When the corner of a field comes into view on the left, turn left, then right, and cross the stream. Continue straight on to the car park.*

1 *Start from the Rufus Stone car park. Cross the road to the Rufus Stone, then walk south-west over the clearing, aiming for the small fenced area. Proceed straight on through a gap in the trees, across a boggy area and up through the grassy glade. Continue straight on where the paths cross.*

3 *About 100 yards (90 m) before the house, turn right through the holly trees and through a clearing, continuing straight on and aiming to the left of the pylon. Head north and follow the path down to the stream.*

2 *Bear right by the concrete drainage outfall and follow the grassy track, which eventually joins a gravel track. Continue on parallel with the A31 towards a white house.*

15

GODSHILL INCLOSURE AND CASTLE HILL

2¾ miles (4½ km) Easy

Here in the north-west, the River Avon butts up against a plateau of high ground that marks the edge of the Forest. The boundary lies along the steep slope facing the river and, from the top, there are marvellous views to the west over the river's lazy meanderings to the chalk country of Cranborne Chase.

This walk certainly offers contrasting scenery, for the view of the heath-covered valley to the east is typical of the Forest. This area was a source of gravel, and the quarrying has exposed the sandy strata responsible for the poor soils of the northern Forest.

The walk through Godshill Inclosure is pleasant, for this is an attractive wood containing a variety of trees, including oak, sweet chestnut, rowan, and various pines.

The nearby village of Woodgreen was once famous for its orchards of sweet black cherries, known as 'Merry Trees'. When the fruit was ripe, people would come from considerable distances to pick them, on occasions which became known as 'Merry Sundays'. These more than lived up to their name, and the day's events often ended in drunken brawls.

Inside the village hall, though, are scenes of peaceful village activities, as captured by two artists in the early 1930s. They painted scenes of Woodgreen in a series of panels, using the villagers as models for the characters, and have portrayed a fairly comprehensive picture of Forest village life half-a-century ago.

A Whoever decided upon this site for their stronghold of Castle Hill fort chose well, for the steep slopes, the River Avon, and the sweeping view would have made this a difficult place to attack. Now, though, the grassy ditches and banks are lent an intimate atmosphere by the surrounding woodland. There is still some uncertainty about their age, but some authorities believe them to be Norman, in which case they would be the only remains of fortifications of that date in the Forest.

Over

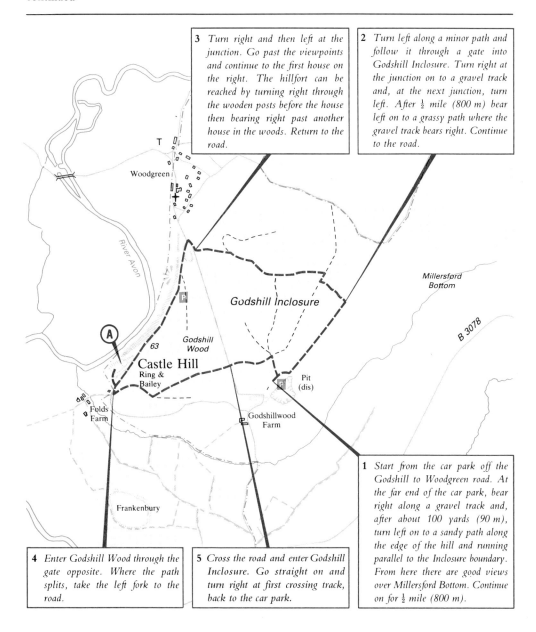

3 Turn right and then left at the junction. Go past the viewpoints and continue to the first house on the right. The hillfort can be reached by turning right through the wooden posts before the house then bearing right past another house in the woods. Return to the road.

2 Turn left along a minor path and follow it through a gate into Godshill Inclosure. Turn right at the junction on to a gravel track and, at the next junction, turn left. After ½ mile (800 m) bear left on to a grassy path where the gravel track bears right. Continue to the road.

1 Start from the car park off the Godshill to Woodgreen road. At the far end of the car park, bear right along a gravel track and, after about 100 yards (90 m), turn left on to a sandy path along the edge of the hill and running parallel to the Inclosure boundary. From here there are good views over Millersford Bottom. Continue on for ½ mile (800 m).

4 Enter Godshill Wood through the gate opposite. Where the path splits, take the left fork to the road.

5 Cross the road and enter Godshill Inclosure. Go straight on and turn right at first crossing track, back to the car park.

17

Walk 3

BISHOP'S DYKE AND DENNY WOOD

3 miles (5 km) Easy

This is an easy stroll through interesting wetlands and some of the New Forest's most beautiful woodland. These diverse habitats support some of the rarer plant and animal species of the area.

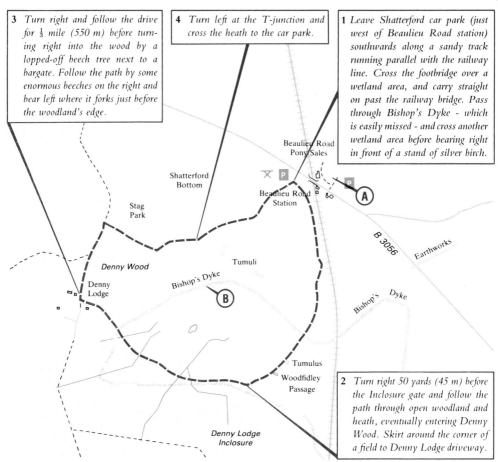

3 *Turn right and follow the drive for ⅓ mile (550 m) before turning right into the wood by a lopped-off beech tree next to a bargate. Follow the path by some enormous beeches on the right and bear left where it forks just before the woodland's edge.*

4 *Turn left at the T-junction and cross the heath to the car park.*

1 *Leave Shatterford car park (just west of Beaulieu Road station) southwards along a sandy track running parallel with the railway line. Cross the footbridge over a wetland area, and carry straight on past the railway bridge. Pass through Bishop's Dyke - which is easily missed - and cross another wetland area before bearing right in front of a stand of silver birch.*

2 *Turn right 50 yards (45 m) before the Inclosure gate and follow the path through open woodland and heath, eventually entering Denny Wood. Skirt around the corner of a field to Denny Lodge driveway.*

Beaulieu Road Pony Sales

Shatterford Bottom

Stag Park

Beaulieu Road Station

B 3056

Earthworks

Denny Wood

Tumuli

Denny Lodge

Bishop's Dyke

Bishop's Dyke

(A)

(B)

Tumulus

Woodfidley Passage

Denny Lodge Inclosure

A The Beaulieu Road pony sales were originally held on Swan Green, Lyndhurst, before being moved to their present location. They are colourful events held five times a year and attract bargain-hunters from all over the country.

B Quite why John de Pontoise, Bishop of Winchester, asked the king in 1284 for permission to enclose 500 acres (200 ha) of boggy waste by a dyke is something of a mystery. It has been suggested, though, that the area was once a lake with ample wildlife for sporting purposes. Local legend has it that the Bishop could only enclose as much land as he could crawl around in a day.

FRITHAM

0 _____ 1 mile

0 _____ 1 km

3¼ miles (5¼ km) Easy; one climb, needs careful route-finding in places

The Dockens Water, clear and hurried at times, flows west from its sources at Fritham through one of the deepest and most beautiful valleys in the Forest. In contrast to the intimate woodland of the valley, Fritham Plain is bare and open, giving good views over the surrounding countryside.

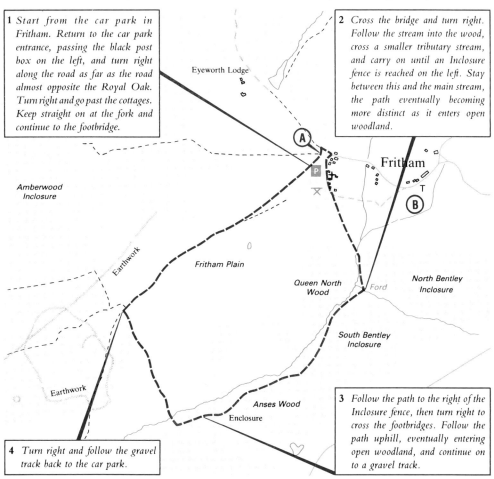

1 *Start from the car park in Fritham. Return to the car park entrance, passing the black post box on the left, and turn right along the road as far as the road almost opposite the Royal Oak. Turn right and go past the cottages. Keep straight on at the fork and continue to the footbridge.*

2 *Cross the bridge and turn right. Follow the stream into the wood, cross a smaller tributary stream, and carry on until an Inclosure fence is reached on the left. Stay between this and the main stream, the path eventually becoming more distinct as it enters open woodland.*

Eyeworth Lodge

Fritham

Amberwood Inclosure

Earthwork

Fritham Plain

Queen North Wood

Ford

North Bentley Inclosure

South Bentley Inclosure

Earthwork

Anses Wood Enclosure

3 *Follow the path to the right of the Inclosure fence, then turn right to cross the footbridges. Follow the path uphill, eventually entering open woodland, and continue on to a gravel track.*

4 *Turn right and follow the gravel track back to the car park.*

A Around the turn of the century, this black letter box was used to receive mail for the gunpowder factory at nearby Eyeworth.

B Recent excavations at Church Green have indicated some sort of settlement here from at least Roman times. The almost radial arrangement of the small fields around the village is typical of medieval cattle farming practice. The Royal Oak is an old pub with walls of wattle and daub.

19

CASTLE HILL AND SMUGGLERS WAY

2¾ miles (4½ km) Easy

The short trudge up the steep slopes of Castle Hill is rewarded by commanding views across the rough heathland that lies on this edge of the Forest. It is an absorbing scene with small ridges and gulleys falling away to the valley below, criss-crossed by the scars of hundreds of years' wear by hoofs and feet. Amid the gorse and heather, self-sown pines dot the heath and dress the occasional hillock. It is an ever-changing picture, too – from the bare browns of winter through to the yellow gorse of early summer and finally the purple blaze of autumn heather.

The sharp-eyed may spot a herd of red deer, our largest wild and native species, for this corner of the Forest is their favourite haunt. But a likelier sighting will be the more abundant fallow deer, with their chestnut summer coats dotted with white.

A Our route climbs from Vales Moor car park to a ridge traversed by the Smugglers Way. For most of its length, it is a grassy swathe but, in its sunken parts, it is not difficult to imagine concealed convoys of men with ponies and wagons loaded with illicit brandy, tea, tobacco, and silk, waiting nervously to hear that H M Customs and Excise had given up the chase.

In the eighteenth and nineteenth centuries, smuggling was both a way of life and big business – big enough to risk transportation or death if caught. It was a time when harsh taxes and meagre wages made a trip across the Channel to pick up heavily taxed luxury items and smuggle them back seem attractive. These brave men in their small sailing boats would face the vagaries of the English Channel and the Revenue cutters before they could disgorge their booty on some dark, secluded beach or inlet. Chewton Bunny, a gully running into the sea at Highcliff, was one such landing point used for cargo destined for Salisbury, Ringwood, Fordingbridge, and Burley, although buyers would sometimes come from as far as Bristol. Ponies and wagons would be loaded up and led inland along secret ways, the men doing their best to avoid often violent skirmishes with Customs' officials. With some of the goods dispersed en route, the procession would probably have passed along Smugglers Way to a remote woodland market, where the remainder would have been sold.

B Lovey Warne and her two brothers were smugglers or 'free traders' living in a cottage at Knave Ash, just west of Vales Moor. When Customs' men were around, she would stand on Verely Hill wearing a bright-red cape to warn other free traders of their presence. At night, a red lantern was hung high in an oak tree.

Over

20

0   1 mile
0   1 km

4 *Where Smugglers Way is joined by a distinct path from behind left, fork right on to a minor path. Continue straight over the crossing track then turn right on to a path down the valley. After ¼ mile (400m), turn left on the distinct path towards Verely Hill and continue to the first junction.*

5 *Turn right and, after 250 yards (230 m), bear right, then bear right again after another 250 yards (230 m). Descend the spur, go under the power lines and pass to the right of a small pond. Continue straight on along a minor path through the gorse back to the car park.*

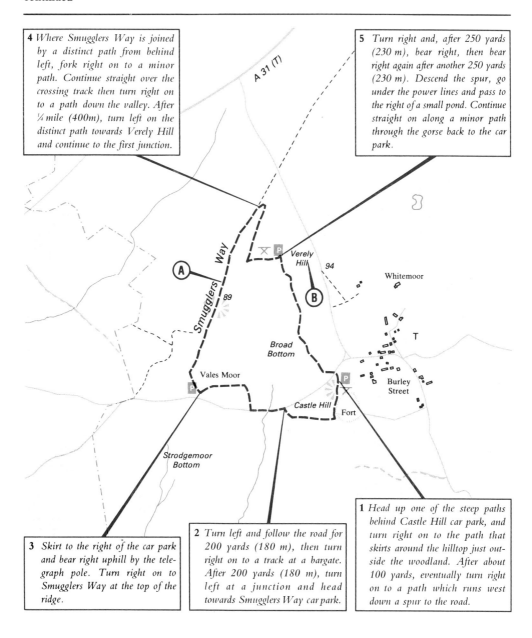

3 *Skirt to the right of the car park and bear right uphill by the telegraph pole. Turn right on to Smugglers Way at the top of the ridge.*

2 *Turn left and follow the road for 200 yards (180 m), then turn right on to a track at a bargate. After 200 yards (180 m), turn left at a junction and head towards Smugglers Way car park.*

1 *Head up one of the steep paths behind Castle Hill car park, and turn right on to the path that skirts around the hilltop just outside the woodland. After about 100 yards, eventually turn right on to a path which runs west down a spur to the road.*

LYMINGTON AND THE SOLENT

5½ miles (9 km) Strenuous; muddy, may be impassable at spring high tides

The New Forest holds many surprises, and its cordial meeting with the sea between the Lymington and Beaulieu estuaries is one of the most pleasant. Just where one ends and the other begins at low tide can be a bit confusing, though not to the thousands of waders and gulls that descend hungrily on to the semiliquid portions to enjoy a rowdy banquet! The going gets a little sticky at times and, on raw days between autumn and spring – when the bird life is at its most interesting – a strong onshore wind can make it bleak, too.

The mudflats are fringed with oaks stunted by centuries of salty gales and, around the high-water mark, scarlet pimpernel, sea campion, thrift, biting stonecrop, and yellow horned poppy can be found. An interesting lagoon provides a home for various waterfowl, including shelduck, while out on the flats, oystercatchers, curlews, lapwings, redshanks, knots, and dunlins are but a few of the birds that can be seen in this area. In fact, 1600 acres (640 ha) of land to the east form the North Solent Nature Reserve, where access is controlled by permit. The area includes Gull Island, where Britain's largest colony of black-headed gulls is found.

The walk begins on the outskirts of Lymington, next to the ferry terminal to Yarmouth on the Isle of Wight. In the fourteenth century, Lymington was building more ships for the navy than Portsmouth, but gradually it became more important for the production of salt.

To the west of the town, the sea was run into shallow pans in the marshes. The sun and wind did their work evaporating much of the water before the brine was finally transferred to coal-fired copper vessels. Salt was a very valuable and taxable commodity extensively used in preserving meat, and the attractive Georgian houses that line the quaint streets of Lymington owe their existence to this lucrative trade. By the mid-nineteenth century, competition from the Cheshire salt mines brought the trade to an end and the town's economy now relies on yachtsmen, tourists, and light industry.

Initially the route is soft going and if the walker's interest lies solely with the shore section then wellingtons may prove more useful than walking boots. For those completing the circular route, however, just persevere, for after about a mile the going improves considerably and the walk ends with a couple of miles walking along quiet roads that form part of the Solent Way.

A On a summer's day, the Solent is a busy place, with boats and ships of all shapes and sizes navigating the 3-mile (4¾-km) wide channel. There are extensive views across to the chalk downs of the Isle of Wight which form part of the rim of the Hampshire basin. On the horizon to the right lies Hurst Castle, situated at the end of a 1½-mile (2½-km) shingle spit. It was built by Henry VIII in 1544 and extensively modified in the early nineteenth century when an invasion by Napoleon seemed imminent. Troops were stationed there during World War 2, and it is now an ancient monument open to the public.

Over

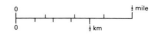

5 *Turn left, then left again by the ferry terminal back to the car.*

4 *Turn left and, after 100 yards (90 m), turn right through a gate on to a waymarked path. Follow this to the road.*

3 *Turn right, then take the first track on the left to a road.*

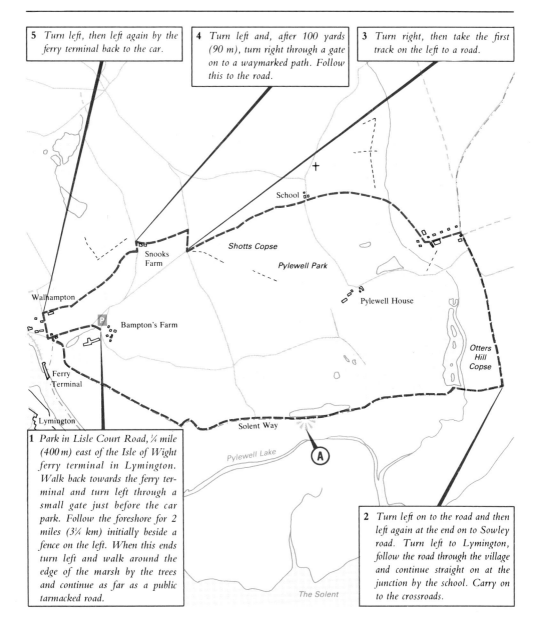

School

Shotts Copse

Snooks Farm

Pylewell Park

Walhampton

Pylewell House

P

Bampton's Farm

Otters Hill Copse

Ferry Terminal

Lymington

Solent Way

A

Pylewell Lake

1 *Park in Lisle Court Road, ¼ mile (400 m) east of the Isle of Wight ferry terminal in Lymington. Walk back towards the ferry terminal and turn left through a small gate just before the car park. Follow the foreshore for 2 miles (3¼ km) initially beside a fence on the left. When this ends turn left and walk around the edge of the marsh by the trees and continue as far as a public tarmacked road.*

2 *Turn left on to the road and then left again at the end on to Sowley road. Turn left to Lymington, follow the road through the village and continue straight on at the junction by the school. Carry on to the crossroads.*

The Solent

23

LINFORD BOTTOM

3¼ miles (5¼ km) Moderate; some mud, compass useful

0   1 mile
0   1 km

This part of the valley cut by the Linford Brook on its way to the Avon is a most attractive spot and is understandably popular with visitors. Do not be deterred by the number of cars in the car park, though, because relatively few people venture beyond the immediate vicinity of their vehicle.

The walk follows the brook upstream through lush Forest lawn and into the pleasant disorder of Pinnick Wood. Hawthorns are unusually abundant here and, together with hollies and bramble, form the understorey for the twisted senile oaks that lend an ancient, timeless quality to the wood.

Surprisingly, one can ignore the busy A31, just ½ mile (800 m) away, but Handy Cross Plain forms a buffer between the tarmac and the woodland. Deer do not seem to mind the traffic and can be seen roaming the heath from inside the wood.

1 *From Linford Bottom car park [about 1 mile (1½ km) north-east of Ringwood], follow the gravel track through a hargate and on up the valley for ½ mile (800 m) to a junction.*

2 *Fork right, following blue way-marks. Do not cross the brook but turn left and follow it upstream to a junction with a gravel track.*

3 *Turn right, cross the bridge, then turn right again in front of the Inclosure gate on to a grassy track. Keep to the right of the boundary fence, then bear slightly right when it turns a corner. Follow the path uphill and out of the wood to a gravel track.*

Red Shoot Wood

Greenford Bottom

Great Linford Inclosure

Linford Brook

Pinnick Wood

Enclosure

Linford Bottom

Little Linford Inclosure

A 31 (T)

Highwood Farm

Linford

5 *Cross the stream and follow the path that approaches tree-lined Linford Brook. Continue down the valley to the left of the brook as far as the road, then turn right across the bridge to the car park.*

4 *Turn sharp right and follow the path downhill. Skirt through the left-hand edge of the wood, eventually emerging by a stream in Linford Bottom.*

Walk 8
NORLEY INCLOSURE
2¼ miles (3½ km) Easy

The trees of Norley Inclosure muffle the noise from the nearby road, and the walker is left to ramble among the seclusion and peace of the trees. It is a pleasant mixed wood, the paths lined with screens of deciduous trees. The walk proceeds through heath and past a typical holly wood or holm, and then along an attractive valley, so there is surprising variety in this short walk.

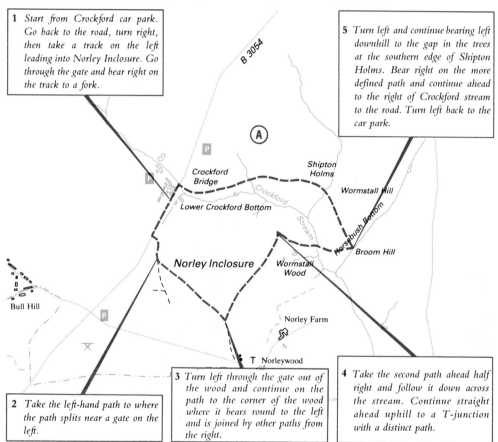

1 *Start from Crockford car park. Go back to the road, turn right, then take a track on the left leading into Norley Inclosure. Go through the gate and bear right on the track to a fork.*

5 *Turn left and continue bearing left downhill to the gap in the trees at the southern edge of Shipton Holms. Bear right on the more defined path and continue ahead to the right of Crockford stream to the road. Turn left back to the car park.*

2 *Take the left-hand path to where the path splits near a gate on the left.*

3 *Turn left through the gate out of the wood and continue on the path to the corner of the wood where it bears round to the left and is joined by other paths from the right.*

4 *Take the second path ahead half right and follow it down across the stream. Continue straight ahead uphill to a T-junction with a distinct path.*

B 3054
Crockford Bridge
Shipton Holms
Wormstall Hill
Lower Crockford Bottom
Crockford
Stream
Horsebush Bottom
Broom Hill
Norley Inclosure
Wormstall Wood
Bull Hill
Norley Farm
Norleywood

A This system of embanked fields is known as the 'Crockford Complex' and covers more than 200 acres (80 ha) of heath. They are probably medieval in origin and the scale of the system is suggestive of estate management rather then individual encroachment into the Forest.

However, fragments of pottery from the first century BC have been unearthed, and there is even evidence of a Bronze Age enclosure, so it is possible that the site was first occupied more than 3000 years ago.

25

BALMER LAWN AND PARK GROUND INCLOSURE

6½ miles (10½ km) Strenuous; some mud, compass useful

This walk lies in the heart of the Forest and explores some of the mass of woodland around Lyndhurst and Brockenhurst. The busy A337 has to be crossed twice and the seemingly endless procession of traffic could be more of an intrusion but, once across the tarmac, the walker is soon deep into the peace of the woods.

The walk begins in an airy, spacious wood among the beautiful old beech and oak trees beside the Lymington river. The open ground to the north is the site of the New Forest Show, held every year in July and an important event in the Forest calendar.

After crossing the road once more, the walker eventually enters Parkhill Inclosure and crosses the remains of a boundary, or Park Pale, of an old royal deer park of some 500 acres (200 ha). This is the site of the Old Park at Lyndhurst, recorded as early as 1291 but which was disparked probably in the sixteenth century. It was superseded by nearby New Park, which became the favourite hunting lodge of Charles II.

Pignal Inclosure, just a little further on, was part of 230 acres (90 ha) first planted in 1756. To the south lies a narrow corridor of open ground stretching from Pignal Hill to Denny Lodge which is used from time to time in the round-up of Commoner's animals.

The combination of the river, inviting grassy banks, and easy access makes this one of the most popular destinations in the Forest.

A The hotel forms an impressive backdrop and is set on Balmer Lawn, approximately 200 acres (80 ha) of open heath that once served as a racecourse for New Forest ponies. Now they are allowed to graze peacefully and help to maintain the lawn in its present state.

The site was the scene of much activity during both world wars. In World War 1, 10 acres (4 ha) of land were enclosed for the establishment of a hospital for wounded Indian troops, to which the King and Queen paid a visit in 1917. Apparently, the hospital was quite an attraction and necessitated the use of barbed wire and sentries to keep out unwelcome visitors.

The area's second moment in history came during World War 2 when the hotel was used by the American Air Force as a command centre during the preparations for the Normandy invasion. They also commandeered the cricket pavilion, which was converted into a post office for the servicemen.

Over

26

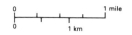

4 Go straight on along the gravel track and, when it goes left into an open glade, bear right on to a path heading north east. After ¼ mile (1¼ km), join a gravel drive and turn right to the road.

5 Turn left along the A337 for 100 yards (90 m), then right into a gateway before the house. Continue straight ahead for ¼ mile (400 m) to a T-junction.

6 Turn left and shortly pass through an Inclosure gate and turn right. Follow the gravel track for ½ mile (800 m) to a gate on the right.

7 Go through the gate and keep on the gravel track. Bear right at the first junction with a gravel track and straight on at the second. Continue to where the track splits into a loop.

8 Turn right down the grassy track then turn left after 100 yards (90 m) on to another grassy track. After ⅓ mile (550 m), continue straight on along a gravel track to Standing Hat car park.

3 Bear right (near a bridge on the left) on to a well-defined path and turn left immediately before the bargate. Go straight on for ¼ mile (400 m) then bear right 100 yards (90 m) before a footbridge, and walk to the left of an Inclosure boundary, eventually meeting a gravel track by a tin hut.

2 Cross the stile and follow the path half-right into the trees, then bear left where it splits after 150 yards (135 m). Go straight on at the next junction and follow the path between the fence and the river.

1 Start from the car park near the Balmer Lawn Hotel, just off the A337 north of Brockenhurst. Cross the Beaulieu road near the cattle grid and follow the sign to Hollands Wood across the lawn. At the campsite entrance, cross the A337 to the stile opposite.

9 Turn right just after the car park, then right again on to a gravel track to the road. Turn right to Balmer Lawn car park.

Lyndhurst

Clayhill

A 35

Park Ground Inclosure

Bishop's Dyke

Hursthill Inclosure

Whitley Wood

A 337

Hollands Wood

Bolderford Bridge

Lymington River

Balmer Lawn

Standing Hat

Balmerlawn

B 3055

Brockenhurst

27

DOCKENS WATER AND SLODEN INCLOSURE

7½ miles (12 km) Strenuous

This walk starts where the road ends, and the walker immediately enters a peaceful and remote part of the Forest away from traffic and crowds.

This is ridge-and-valley country offering a pleasant scenic variety of wooded ridges, heather-covered hillsides, and damp, lush lowland. There is also an amazing variety of trees on this walk. In Broomy Inclosure, there are beautiful oaks, many of them encircled by thick coils of ivy. In Sloden there is an unusual combination of yew, whitebeam, and ash, and, in Hasley Inclosure, sweet chestnut accompanies the conifers.

Hasley Inclosure once consisted mainly of chestnut, which thrives on the sandy soil. This is a startling deep-red colour, stained by the presence of iron which also occurs nearby as limonite. This was excavated by the local potters in Roman times for use in their kilns.

The walk also crosses the lovely valley of Dockens Water, and the view from the river upwards to Sloden over the curiously named Ragged Boys Hill is a most attractive scene.

A If you feel there is something different about the atmosphere in Sloden Inclosure it is probably due to the presence of the sombre yews, a tree somewhat unexpected in New Forest woodland and which was once much more extensive here. It was probably planted no earlier than the eighteenth century.

There was a coppice in Elizabethan times, and there still remains some 67½ acres (27 ha) of eighteenth-century plantation. Sloden is noted for its variety of trees, for, as well as the yew, there is oak, holly, hawthorn, and whitebeam while the ash is more abundant here than anywhere else in the Forest.

The availability of suitable raw materials in this north-western part of the Forest led to the growth of a pottery industry in Romano-British times. Sloden was one of these sites, producing distinctive 'New Forest Ware' which has been unearthed on Roman sites throughout the country.

Heywood Sumner excavated in Sloden and his best finds are now in the British Museum. He found no coins and surmises that a barter economy would have existed during this period, some time in the third and fourth centuries AD. He comments that the Sloden pottery was less refined and probably of an earlier date than those finds made at kilns in Islands Thorns, Crock Hill, and Ashley Rails.

Over

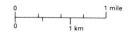

5 *Go through the gate and turn left on to the ride. Bear slightly right at the wood's edge and keep to a path to the left of Latchmore Brook as far as a well-made gravel road.*

4 *Loop around to the left and re-enter the Inclosure through the gate. Follow the gravel track for ¼ mile (1¼ km) to a junction and bear right (there is a gate to open land on the left). Continue downhill past the next junction to the Inclosure gate.*

3 *Cross the bridge and follow the track uphill into Sloden Inclosure. Stay on it until it leaves the woodland.*

6 *Turn left and follow the track between farmland. Bear left at the Partridge Piece sign, then bear right past the farm.*

7 *Bear left at the fork, go through the Inclosure gate, then turn left. Follow the track around the Inclosure and turn left at the junction, leaving the wood through the gate and continuing on to a junction.*

8 *Turn right on to a sandy path and follow it downhill across Splash Bridge. Turn right and follow the grassy track between Dockens Water and the Inclosure boundary back to the car park.*

1 *Park in Woodford Bottom car park at the end of the long gravel track, past the High Corner Inn, from the minor road between Lyndhurst and Ringwood. Go straight on from the car park, following the track through the gate into Broomy Inclosure. Carry on for about 1 mile (1½ km), passing through another gate and eventually reaching a crossing of gravel tracks.*

2 *Turn left and follow the track down to the river, past Holly Hatch Cottage to the bridge.*

Islands Thorns Inclosure

B 3078

Earthwork

Frogham

Sloden Inclosure

Latchmore   Brook

Earthwork

P

Ogdens

Hasley Hill

Splash Bridge

Water

A

Holly Hatch Inclosure

Holly Hatch Cottage

Dockens

Woodford Bottom

Broomy Inclosure

Broomy Lodge

High Corner Inn

A 338

R. Avon

A 31 (T)

29

BEAULIEU AND BUCKLERS HARD

4¾ miles (7½ km) Moderate

This is not true forest in the sense of open heath and woodland, for the land bordering the Solent and Beaulieu river is privately owned and extensively farmed, with few public rights of way. Nevertheless, this walk follows a trail through maritime history, alongside one of the most beautiful and relatively unspoilt estuaries in England.

Jarvis's Copse is dissected by a small creek and is a particularly interesting patch of woodland. It is a haven for wild flowers – look out in the summer for the shredded pink flowers of ragged robin, butterfly and spotted orchids, and several varieties of vetch.

A circular route requires the use of public roads which can be very busy in the high season, so the walker may wish to return from Bucklers Hard by the outward route.

A Mention Beaulieu to most people and they will immediately think of vintage motor cars, boat and auto jumbles. Indeed, few people venture south of the gates to Lord Montagu's leisure park – where the National Motor Museum is housed – to Beaulieu village itself. This red-brick village is seen at its best from the B3054 by the disused seventeenth-century tide mill.

The land for Beaulieu Abbey was granted to the Cistercian Order by King John in 1204, and a great empire of prayer and commerce grew up with the fine Abbey buildings. The monks were prolific farmers and produced much wool and grain for export. The village expanded around the Abbey but the monks' appetite for grazing land often brought them into conflict with the local people.

Unfortunately, most of the Abbey was destroyed during the Reformation with only the refectory remaining intact; this was later converted into the parish church. The gatehouse was turned into a dwelling which has been used by Lord Montagu's family since 1538. Much of the ruined stone was shipped off for use in coastal defences such as Hurst Castle.

B Naval shipbuilding on the Beaulieu estuary started at Bailey's Hard in 1698 with the construction of the *Salisbury* and finished in World War 2 with the construction of a wooden minesweeper. Parts of the Mulberry floating harbour, which played such a vital role in the Normandy landings of 1944, were also constructed on the far side of the estuary, in deep channels originally intended for oyster farming.

C It is difficult to imagine that this spot, remote from any sizeable town, was once a centre of shipbuilding. In the eighteenth century, however, the industry required square miles of forest rather than acres of belching furnaces to provide the bulk of the raw materials.

A small warship such as Nelson's *Agamemnon*, built in 1781, would require about 2000 mature oaks from the Forest for its construction, along with beech, elm, and imported pine.

The wide street of Bucklers Hard, now a grassy lawn, would once have been stacked high with seasoning timber. Ships were built at the bottom of the street and launched straight into the deep water channel. These were times of great celebration, attended by thousands of local people. The bare hulls would then be towed to Portsmouth to be fitted out and have their masts stepped.

About fifty vessels were built here between 1745 and 1809, mostly under the direction of master shipbuilder, Henry Adams. His house is now a hotel, and one of the village cottages houses the Beaulieu Maritime Museum, where the history of boatbuilding on the estuary is told in graphic detail.

It is interesting to note that Bucklers Hard almost became a sugar refinery. In the 1740s, John, Second Duke of Beaulieu, planned to import sugarcane from the West Indies and refine it using abundant Forest fuel. Montagu Town was to be built at Bucklers Hard to house refinery workers. However, the supplying islands were lost to the French and the plan abandoned in favour of shipbuilding.

Over

0 ⊢———————————————⊣ 1 mile
0 ⊢———————————————⊣ 1 km

1 *Start from the free car park in Beaulieu and walk to the main street along the gravel path. Turn left.*

2 *Just after the Montagu Arms, turn right down a signposted footpath, past the fire station and continue on to a stile.*

3 *Cross the stile and follow the path straight on over the fields to a small creek.*

4 *Go through the barrier, follow the creek inland, then cross it and pass through Jarvis's Copse. Pass through the barrier and follow the left-hand field boundary to Bailey's Hard.*

5 *At the cottage cross the stile into Bailey's Hard. Bear right on the drive and after about 100 yards on a sharp right hand bend cut off left along the footpath. Cross the footbridge and continue to the river, following the clear path eventually to a junction with gravel track.*

6 *Turn left and continue around the back of the marina to the car park. Turn left on the footpath signposted for Buckler's Hard.*

7 *Return through the same car park and pick up the path once more behind the marina as far as the next car park. This time continue straight along the gravel track to Bailey's Hard and retrace the outward route back to Beaulieu.*

Motor Museum

Abbey Remains of (Cistercian founded 1204)

Palace House

B 3056

Beaulieu

T

Ⓐ

B 3054

Bunker's Farm

Jarvis's Copse

Beufre Farm

Oxleys Copse

River

Bailey's Hard

Beaulieu

Ⓑ

Keeping Copse

Keeping Marsh

Ashen Wood

Keeping

Keeping Farm

Bucklers Hard

Ⓒ

T

P

31

BRAMSHAW WOOD AND PIPER'S WAIT

2¾ miles (4½ km) Easy; a compass is useful

The walk begins and ends among the shelter of the beautiful Ancient and Ornamental Wood at Bramshaw, with a section of exposed heathland between. The plateau at Piper's Wait reaches a height of 422 feet (129 m) - the highest point in the Forest, with good views to the north over Wiltshire and to the west towards Bramshaw Telegraph. To greatly add to your enjoyment of this route, make sure you get off to a good start and pick up the right path from the car park. Some very simple compass work will send you easily on your way for a most rewarding walk.

A Bramshaw Wood has been classed by the Nature Conservancy as a 'forest nature reserve'. It was not enclosed until 1829, but the area has been wooded for much longer than that - its Saxon name means a wood containing much bramble. In the thirteenth century the woods provided timber for the building of Salisbury Cathedral. They were also shelters for smugglers and one of the last sites to be occupied by gypsies.

B The curious name of Nomansland is due to its position across the county boundaries of Hampshire and Wiltshire which, in this instance, also happens to define the edge of the Forest. This line is also followed by the main street and is said to split the Lamb Inn in Wiltshire from its front step lying in Hampshire!

There was frequent confusion as to whether or not the village lay in the Forest and, until 1800, any squatter wishing to establish himself by building a house would have his home pulled down by the authorities. In 1800, however, the decision was made by the Commissioners to allow building to take place and forty years later, there were forty-two houses recorded in the village. The people formed a tough, independent community and managed to avoid paying county rates in the middle of the nineteenth century by intimidating the collector!

Over

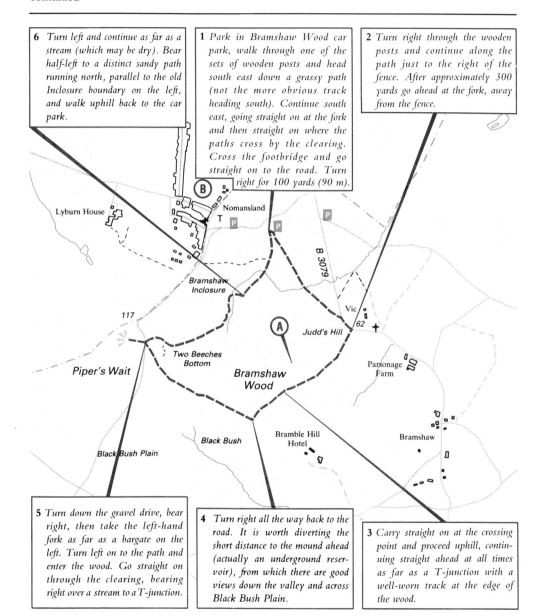

6 Turn left and continue as far as a stream (which may be dry). Bear half-left to a distinct sandy path running north, parallel to the old Inclosure boundary on the left, and walk uphill back to the car park.

1 Park in Bramshaw Wood car park, walk through one of the sets of wooden posts and head south east down a grassy path (not the more obvious track heading south). Continue south east, going straight on at the fork and then straight on where the paths cross by the clearing. Cross the footbridge and go straight on to the road. Turn right for 100 yards (90 m).

2 Turn right through the wooden posts and continue along the path just to the right of the fence. After approximately 300 yards go ahead at the fork, away from the fence.

Lyburn House

Nomansland

Bramshaw Inclosure

117

B 3079

Vic
62

Judd's Hill

Piper's Wait

Two Beeches Bottom

Bramshaw Wood

Parsonage Farm

Black Bush

Bramble Hill Hotel

Bramshaw

Black Bush Plain

5 Turn down the gravel drive, bear right, then take the left-hand fork as far as a bargate on the left. Turn left on to the path and enter the wood. Go straight on through the clearing, bearing right over a stream to a T-junction.

4 Turn right all the way back to the road. It is worth diverting the short distance to the mound ahead (actually an underground reservoir), from which there are good views down the valley and across Black Bush Plain.

3 Carry straight on at the crossing point and proceed uphill, continuing straight ahead at all times as far as a T-junction with a well-worn track at the edge of the wood.

HOLMSLEY INCLOSURE

3 miles (5 km) Easy; muddy in places

The name of the Inclosure indicates that the holly was once more abundant – 'holm' is an old word for holly – although now the population is much depleted. Indeed, a survey on New Forest coppices in 1609 records that, even at that date, the hollies were old and not particularly abundant.

It was planted in 1811 with oak and Scots pine but there are also birch, sweet chestnut, yew and, of course, the conifers.

Just outside the Inclosure is an interesting area of boggy land and its associated flora. Here, the presence of oaks and marsh form a somewhat strange combination.

5 *Go through the gate and continue to a gravel track. Turn left and go straight on uphill to the road. Turn left back to the car park.*

1 *Start from the car park near Holmsley Lodge. Leave by the path to the left of a large holly tree at the bottom of the car park and go downhill to the corner of the Inclosure.*

2 *Turn right and follow a path along the Inclosure boundary, eventually crossing some footbridges, as far as the entrance of the sawmill.*

4 *Turn right and shortly leave the wood over a stile. Turn right and follow the Inclosure boundary to a gate.*

3 *Turn right through the sawmill and into Holmsley Inclosure. Carry straight on, cross the road, and enter the Inclosure opposite. Follow the gravel track for 1 mile (1½ km), ignoring all tracks off it, until a T-junction with a track.*

A Holmsley airfield was opened in 1942, one of three to be built in the Forest. During World War 2, the Forest was a training area for the troops preparing for the D-Day landings, and the airfield played an important role in the invasion of Europe in 1944. It was closed in 1946 and, in 1964, became the first organized campsite in the Forest.

Walk 14
KING'S HAT INCLOSURE
AND BEAULIEU HEATH
$2\frac{1}{4}$ miles ($3\frac{1}{2}$ km) Easy

This is a short but varied walk through Inclosures containing both coniferous and deciduous woodland, and open sandy heathland.

In Foxhunting Inclosure, look out for beech, oak, holly, sweet chestnut, birch, and Scots pine. Once on the heath, the south-eastern skyline is filled with the metallic flues and stacks of Fawley refinery, pointing skywards like a row of discordant organ pipes. An unwelcome intrusion perhaps, but they may have played a vital part in getting you to the car park!

'Hat' is a Forest term used to describe a prominent group of trees, often 'capping' a hilltop.

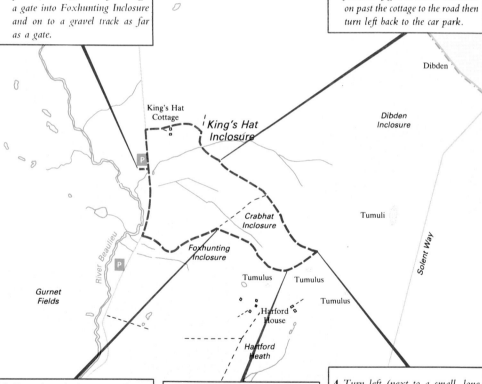

1 From the car park go back to the road and turn right. After 500 yards (450 m), turn left through a gate into Foxhunting Inclosure and on to a gravel track as far as a gate.

5 Pass through the gate into King's Hat Inclosure and turn left at the junction of gravel tracks. Continue on past the cottage to the road then turn left back to the car park.

2 Pass through the gate and turn right up the ride. Keep to the left-hand fence and when the wood ends follow the path straight on over the heathland.

3 Just before the junction with a broad track from the right, take a small path through the heather on the left to a junction with a broad sandy path.

4 Turn left (next to a small, lone pine). Pass to the right of the Inclosure boundary and go straight on at the junction with a wide gravel track.

Map labels: Dibden, Dibden Inclosure, King's Hat Cottage, King's Hat Inclosure, P, Crabhat Inclosure, Tumuli, Solent Way, River Beaulieu, P, Foxhunting Inclosure, Gurnet Fields, Tumulus, Tumulus, Tumulus, Harford House, Harford Heath

MINSTEAD AND FURZEY GARDENS

2¼ miles (3½ km) Easy

This is an easy walk that brings rich returns for the relatively small amount of physical exertion involved. It passes through a lovely Forest village with an unusual church and on to internationally renowned gardens that also contain within their confines an interesting and well-preserved 400-year-old cottage.

Minstead is recorded in Domesday Book as 'Mintestede' – mint place – a Saxon name that reflects the importance of the locally abundant herb at that time. It was used as an air freshener to counteract the heady mixture of human bodies, dogs, and food scraps that found their way on to the floors of the dwellings.

Facing the attractive village green is the Trusty Servant Inn and its curious sign. The design was copied from a seventeenth-century original in Winchester College and sold to the innkeeper by the artist. The character is a composition of several animals, and depicts discretion, patience, and swiftness while the tools and weapons represent a willingness to labour and defend the master – all deemed as virtues in the ideal and trusted servant.

A The first thing most people notice about Minstead's church is its unusual homely appearance – with its dormer windows set among the roof tiles, it resembles more of a cottage leaning against a tower. It is first recorded in 1272, but parts of the building are definitely earlier than this.

Stone was only used for the arches and cornerstones, with the rest of the building constructed of the traditional Forest wattle and daub, covered with lime plaster. Parts of the structure, though, appear to have been strengthened by the shells of oysters. These were the perquisites of the masons and were possibly obtained from beds at Lymington.

The curious exterior is matched by the unusual interior features, notably the private pews used by the various local families. That of the Castle Malwood family, for instance, has comfortable seats and even a fireplace. There are two galleries at the western end, the upper section probably meant to seat the poor and the charity school children.

The stone font with its crude carvings is thought to be Saxon and, until 1893, remained buried in the rectory garden. The rarest feature of the church, though, is the seventeenth-century three-decker pulpit. The lower deck was used by the parish clerk for the 'Amens', while the middle and upper decks were used for scripture readings and sermons.

In the churchyard is the grave of Sir Arthur Conan Doyle, who owned a cottage in the parish, at Bignell Wood. He featured Minstead in his book *The White Company*.

B Furzey gardens were originally designed and planted in 1922 on a site that had to be transformed from rough gorse grazing land by many cartloads of imported soil. There are now 8 acres (3¼ ha) of gardens containing plants, trees, and shrubs from all over the world.

The gardens are particularly noted for their collection of heathers and the massed displays of flowers at particular times of the year – crocus, snowdrops, daffodils, and bluebells in the spring and azaleas and rhododendrons in the summer. There is a comprehensive collection of British ferns, and several varieties of fish are stocked in the pond. Furzey House was built in 1922 and is said to have the longest thatched roof in Hampshire.

The cottage at the entrance to the gardens provides a fascinating insight into the living conditions of the foresters as they existed around the turn of the century. It was built in 1560, the roof beams and upstairs floorboards composed of timbers originating from the Tudor shipyard at Lymington. Access to the two small bedrooms was by a ladder and it seems incredible that the cottage once housed a family of fourteen children! The last of the family was buried at Minstead in 1976.

Over

0   1 mile

0   1 km

5 *Take the right-hand fork, go through a wooden barrier and continue straight on to a junction with a track. Turn left to Furzey Gardens car park and on to a junction.*

6 *Turn right as far as a triangular green, then turn right for 250 yards (230 m) to a stile on the left. Cross the stile and follow the path along the edge of the fields to the road. Turn right back to Minstead.*

1 *Park in the car park opposite The Trusty Servant and turn left in front of the pub along the road to the church. Coming out of the church, turn left at the lychgate, then left again through a gate on to a path. Follow this through the wood on to a dirt track, then turn right to the road.*

A 31 (T)

Malwood Castle
Fort

Malwood

Seaman's Corner

London
Minstead

Minstead
Hall

Home
Farm

Minstead Lodge

The Grove

Furzey (B)

Minstead

T

P

King's Garn

Newtown

Park
Farm

Woodside

T

Manor Wood

(A)

3 *Turn right and continue until the road bends sharp right by Oakleaf Cottage. Go over the stile to the left of the drive, cross the next stile and carry on up the left hand edge of the field to the stile ahead.*

4 *Cross this and then turn immediately right at the waymarked post. Cross the stile and footbridge and carry on to a wooden barrier in the fence on the right.*

2 *Turn left, cross the stream, and continue straight on at the junction as far as a triangular green.*

MARK ASH WOOD

2¾ miles (4½ km) Easy

The New Forest contains much beautiful woodland and most visitors have their personal favourites. It would be pointless, therefore, to pick out one wood that is outstanding above the rest, but certainly Mark Ash must count as one of the most attractive, and it is but a short distance from the car park to the heart of the woodland.

One of the first impressions of the wood is that it has been left to the vagaries of nature. This is not quite true, of course, but the apparent disarray and the consequent richness of flora and fauna offer a pleasing contrast to the severe rows of conifers elsewhere in the Forest. The fallen and decaying trees provide food and home for a variety of insects, ferns, and fungi, while the ground is covered with cushions of hummocky moss carpet. These are characteristic features of beechwoods and lend a startling brightness to the comparative gloom of the forest floor.

Another feature of this wood are the huge pollarded beeches that stand in isolated majesty among the younger trees. Since pollarding was declared illegal in 1698, these trees are known to be at least 300 years old.

The stream in the valley is lined with alder, a tree that was frequently coppiced and that was important for charcoal during the two world wars. The original ash tree included in the name of the wood, however, has long since disappeared. It was marked in some way and acted as a boundary feature to one of the settlements in the Forest nearby.

Over

0   1 mile

0   1 km

4 *Turn left along the grassy path and continue straight ahead between the fences to a crossing of tracks.*

3 *Turn left, cross the stream, and follow the track past some magnificent pollarded beeches to the road. Go straight across along the track (note the beech bough seemingly both rooted and branched on the left!) over a footbridge as far as an Inclosure gate.*

2 *Turn left and after 350 yards (300 m) take the left-hand fork between the conifers, through the gate and into Mark Ash Wood. Follow the fence on the right until it ends near a junction with a grassy track.*

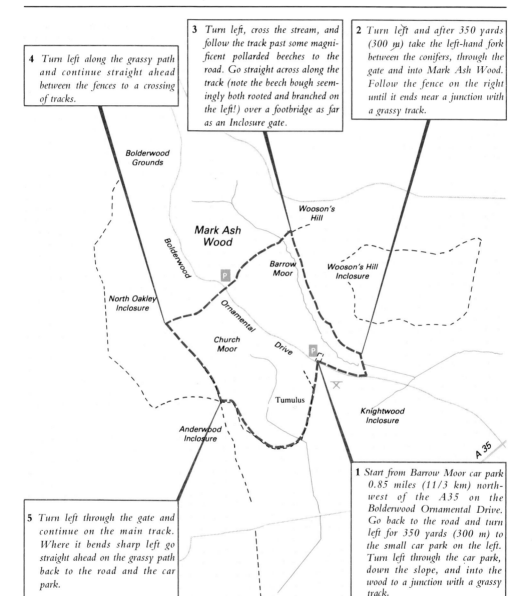

Bolderwood
Grounds

Wooson's
Hill

*Mark Ash
Wood*

Bolderwood

Barrow
Moor

Wooson's Hill
Inclosure

North Oakley
Inclosure

Ornamental

Church
Moor

Drive

Tumulus

Knightwood
Inclosure

Anderwood
Inclosure

A 35

5 *Turn left through the gate and continue on the main track. Where it bends sharp left go straight ahead on the grassy path back to the road and the car park.*

1 *Start from Barrow Moor car park 0.85 miles (11/3 km) north-west of the A35 on the Bolderwood Ornamental Drive. Go back to the road and turn left for 350 yards (300 m) to the small car park on the left. Turn left through the car park, down the slope, and into the wood to a junction with a grassy track.*

39

WILVERLEY PLAIN

4½ miles (7¼ km) Moderate; two climbs, some mud

This is a good, varied ramble with a splendid sense of isolation. It begins on the playing-field-like expanse of Wilverley Plain, and the walk down through the heather of Hincheslea Moor takes you among an interesting tangle of rivers and streams before heading up through some primeval-looking woodland, finally returning across the heath to Wilverley Plain. Hincheslea Moor, like many of the heaths, is a good place to see birds of prey that hunt in open spaces. These include the kestrel (the only bird that regularly hovers), the hobby, and the buzzard.

The buzzard is a large bird with rounded wingtips that soars effortlessly in thermals over the Forest. Its diet includes small rabbits, reptiles, squirrels, and some large birds. The kestrel feeds mainly on insects, small mammals, and reptiles which, like the larger prey of the buzzard, are not particularly abundant in the Forest.

Consequently, the population densities of these birds here are lower than those in other parts of the country.

The hobby is of similar size to the kestrel but has much darker and stronger markings with a distinctive red-brown coloration on the male's legs. It lives on large insects and small birds caught on the wing and survives relatively well in the Forest.

A There are excellent views from Hincheslea Moor over the southern Forest. The large conifers, standing head and shoulders above the rest of the trees on the northern skyline, are the North American species planted in the 1850s alongside what is now Rhinefield Ornamental Drive. These are now some of the largest trees in Britain.

Over

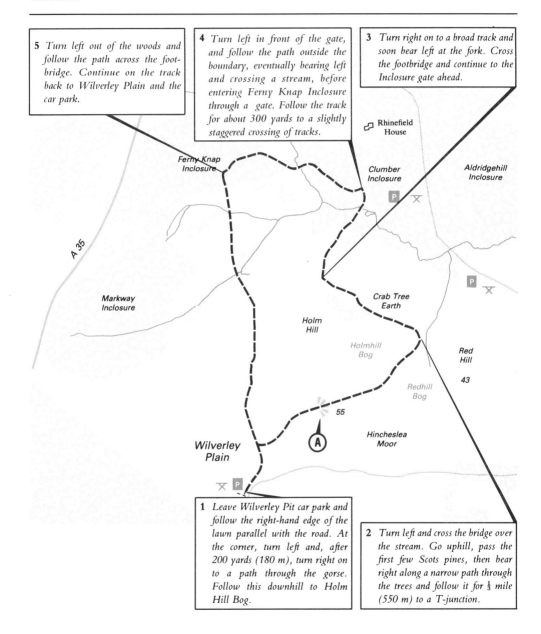

5 *Turn left out of the woods and follow the path across the foot-bridge. Continue on the track back to Wilverley Plain and the car park.*

4 *Turn left in front of the gate, and follow the path outside the boundary, eventually bearing left and crossing a stream, before entering Ferny Knap Inclosure through a gate. Follow the track for about 300 yards to a slightly staggered crossing of tracks.*

3 *Turn right on to a broad track and soon bear left at the fork. Cross the footbridge and continue to the Inclosure gate ahead.*

Rhinefield House

Ferny Knap Inclosure

Clumber Inclosure

Aldridgehill Inclosure

A 35

Markway Inclosure

Crab Tree Earth

Holm Hill

Holmhill Bog

Red Hill

43

Redhill Bog

55

(A)

Wilverley Plain

Hincheslea Moor

1 *Leave Wilverley Pit car park and follow the right-hand edge of the lawn parallel with the road. At the corner, turn left and, after 200 yards (180 m), turn right on to a path through the gorse. Follow this downhill to Holm Hill Bog.*

2 *Turn left and cross the bridge over the stream. Go uphill, pass the first few Scots pines, then bear right along a narrow path through the trees and follow it for ½ mile (550 m) to a T-junction.*

41

DARK WATER

5 miles (8 km) Moderate

Here, in the most easterly part of the Forest, the Dark Water has cut a lovely peaceful valley through the woods on its way to the Solent.

It is a walk of considerable contrasts for it seems impossible to believe, while walking through the tranquility of King's Copse, that just 2 miles (3¼ km) away lies the industrial mass of Fawley refinery.

This is one of the largest refining and chemical manufacturing sites in Europe, employing just over 2000 people. The developed site occupies 1250 acres (500 ha) with almost 500 tanks dotting the landscape. The marine terminal in Southampton Water is almost a mile (1½ km) long and handles around 2500 ships a year.

It was first developed in the 1920s, taking advantage of the deep and sheltered anchorage nearby, and has since attracted other related industries to the site. About 60 per cent of the crude oil comes from the North Sea, and the finished products leave the refinery mainly by sea or pipeline – there are direct pipeline links to Heathrow, Gatwick, Avonmouth, and the Midlands.

A The tumuli form distinct hillocks on the flat heath, and break up the otherwise level contours of the land. They are thought to date from the Bronze Age and are now somewhat eroded, but enough remains of the largest to give an indication of the original size of the burial mounds and the amount of work that must have gone into their construction.

B This was the site of Holbury Manor, held in medieval times by the monks of Beaulieu. Little remains now, although the moat can still be traced.

But the area has a longer history of settlement for it was known to be occupied in Roman times, while the discovery of Mesolithic and Neolithic flints hint at human presence millennia before that.

Over

0   1 mile

0   1 km

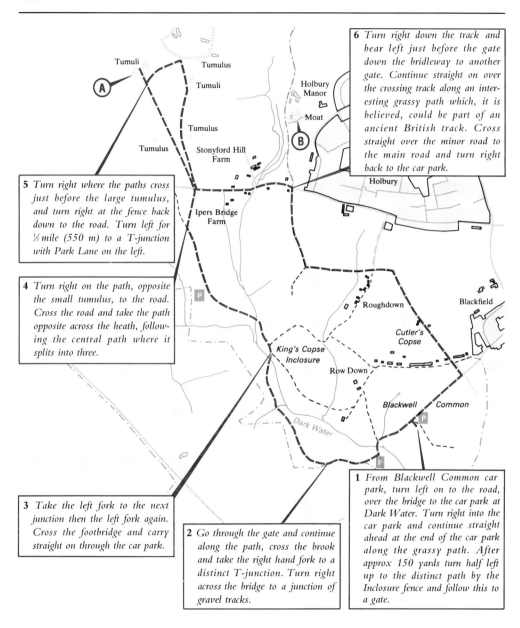

Tumuli

Tumulus

(A)

Tumuli

Holbury
Manor

Moat

Tumulus

(B)

Tumulus

Stonyford Hill
Farm

Holbury

6 Turn right down the track and bear left just before the gate down the bridleway to another gate. Continue straight on over the crossing track along an interesting grassy path which, it is believed, could be part of an ancient British track. Cross straight over the minor road to the main road and turn right back to the car park.

5 Turn right where the paths cross just before the large tumulus, and turn right at the fence back down to the road. Turn left for ⅓ mile (550 m) to a T-junction with Park Lane on the left.

Ipers Bridge
Farm

4 Turn right on the path, opposite the small tumulus, to the road. Cross the road and take the path opposite across the heath, following the central path where it splits into three.

P

Roughdown

Blackfield

Cutler's
Copse

King's Copse
Inclosure

Row Down

Dark Water

Blackwell   Common

P

P

3 Take the left fork to the next junction then the left fork again. Cross the footbridge and carry straight on through the car park.

2 Go through the gate and continue along the path, cross the brook and take the right hand fork to a distinct T-junction. Turn right across the bridge to a junction of gravel tracks.

1 From Blackwell Common car park, turn left on to the road, over the bridge to the car park at Dark Water. Turn right into the car park and continue straight ahead at the end of the car park along the grassy path. After approx 150 yards turn half left up to the distinct path by the Inclosure fence and follow this to a gate.

CASTLE HILL, WHITTEN POND, AND BURLEY

5¾ miles (9¼ km) Moderate

On this walk, there are good views, an attractive Forest village, and interesting wildlife – both real and mythical! – enough variety to suit most tastes.

The heathland flora and fauna are typical of the Forest, including purple bell heather and, in the wetter areas, the pink cross-leaved heath. There are also common and heath-spotted orchids while very close to the ground, are the bright-blue flowers of milkwort. This is also the home of the rare Dartford warbler. It has a soft churring note, a grey back, and a long tail, but its most distinctive feature is a red ring around its eye.

Features of this walk are the ponds that dot the heath. They attract their own range of plants and animals, including the delicate bog pimpernel and water plantain, unusual for its three-petalled flowers. Whitten Pond is a very restful spot, often surrounded by ponies and cattle. On a hot summer day – with a little bit of imagination – it can look like a waterhole on the African savanna.

A Castle Hill lies at the northern end of a ridge that overlooks the Avon valley, Dorset, and Wiltshire. In the past, the site has been excavated for gravel and the workings, together with the trees, largely obscure the outline of the circular earthworks. It is a good site for a stronghold, for the ground falls away steeply on three sides, and it appears that the place was the scene of several battles.

Further south along the ridge is Burley Beacon where a Bronze Age axe and Roman coins were discovered in the 1920s. It is also a place of legend for it is said to have been the lair of the Bisterne Dragon, a beast that reputedly devoured men and cattle in the locale. The hero of this fifteenth-century tale is Sir Maurice Berkeley, who was the only man able to overcome the dragon. Sadly, he lost his life in the process and his death is recorded – he actually did exist – in 1460. It is possible that the beast was one of the last remaining wolves, magnified by legend into an awesome monster.

B Burley is a scattered village but was originally centred around the Manor House. The first Great House was built in the thirteenth century by Richard de Burley but this was pulled down in 1780 and replaced with a Georgian building complete with park and lake. This burned down in 1850 and was replaced by an Elizabethan-style building which is now the Burley Manor Hotel. This was used by American troops during World War 2.

The oldest building in the village is said to be the Queen's Head, whose first publican began serving ale in 1699. Inside, it certainly looks the part with its low ceilings, beams, and relics of yesteryear. There are strong reminders of Burley's connection with smuggling – a link recently reinforced with the discovery of a hidden cellar containing pistols, bottles, and old coins.

Over

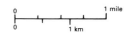

2 *Turn right on to the track and pass the houses. Where the fenced area on the right ends, turn right immediately and follow a minor path downhill to a junction with a well-worn path.*

1 *Park in the car park at the foot of Castle Hill. Climb one of the steep paths behind the car park and turn right on to a path that skirts around the hill, just outside the woodland. Continue as far as a well-made gravel track.*

7 *Turn right on to the road and then left into the drive of Burley Hill House. Pass through the small gate to the right of the main gate and follow the fenced path through the woodland. Go straight on at the end of the fenced path, turn right once more on the well-made gravel track, and retrace the route back to the car park.*

3 *Turn left on to the path and continue in a southerly direction, going straight on through the copse and ignoring the minor paths either side. Eventually, pass to the left of a large pond before meeting the road next to a disused railway line.*

Burley New
Inclosure

Castle
Hill

A

Fort

T

Burley
Street

Strodgemoor
Bottom

Burley
Hill

Burley

T

Bisterne
Close

Dismantled Railway

B

Shappen

Turf
Hill

A 35

Holmsley Walk

Whitten
Pond

Holmsley
Ridge

Wilverley
Inclosure

Holmsley
Inclosure

4 *Turn right on to the road, cross the bridge, then go half-left along a well-defined path which passes to the right of Whitten Pond. Follow the clearly defined path uphill on to Holmsley Ridge, eventually passing to the left of a fenced quarry.*

5 *Continue past the quarry, keeping parallel to the quarry track for approx 200 yards, then take the left fork in the path and continue downhill. Cross the disused railway track next to the old bridge and carry straight on up Turf Hill, passing to the left of a golf course before meeting the road.*

6 *Turn left into Burley and then turn right at the memorial cross. After approximately ¼ mile (400 m), look for the footpath on the right-hand side signposted to Burley Street, and follow this until it rejoins the road.*

BOLTON'S BENCH AND MATLEY WOOD

5¼ miles (8½ km) Moderate

The walk starts and finishes just outside Lyndhurst, long held to be the 'capital' of the Forest. Its Saxon name reflects a period of time when the lime, or linden tree, was once much more common in the Forest.

Lyndhurst is a busy town, with traffic from several major roads channelled around its one-way system but it is, nevertheless, an historic place. It has long had royal associations and some of its traditions and customs are distinctly medieval.

There was a royal manor here in the tenth century, on an important site at the junction of routes radiating out to Beaulieu, Southampton, Christchurch and Lymington. There are records ordering timber for the 'Queen's Manor House' in the thirteenth century, but the present Queen's House was largely rebuilt in the seventeenth century. It was used by Charles II and James II but was ignored by royalty after George III.

It later became the residence of the Warden of the Forest and then the Deputy Surveyor, but now houses the offices of the Forestry Commission. It is an imposing brick building at the western end of the town.

Adjoining is the Verderers' Hall, another very historical building dating from 1388 but much altered since. This place is rich in Forest history and tradition, for the Verderers' Court has sat here since the fourteenth century, solving disputes and dispensing justice within the Forest boundaries.

The Court meets here on a Monday every two months and the sessions are open to the public. Should you choose to attend you will notice an unusually large stirrup iron – it measures 10½ by 7½ inches (26.7 by 19 cm). Known as the 'Rufus Stirrup', it was supposedly used to ascertain those dogs liable to the medieval law of 'expedition', whereby three claws were cut from the

forefeet to prevent the dog from chasing the deer. Those animals small enough to pass through were exempt from this cruel act, a reminder of the brutality of the old Forest laws. In reality, though, the stirrup is probably of Tudor or seventeenth-century date.

Away from the noise of the town, the walk proceeds through the heath to the beautiful old wood at Matley and on to an interesting wetter area with its associated flora. Among the flowers to be found here are bog pimpernel, bog asphodel, and sundew. The last named plant is one of several insectivorous species in the Forest that make up for the lack of nitrogen in the soil by absorbing it from the bodies of insects. These are caught on the sticky substance at the ends of the hairs covering the leaves, which then fold over to trap the insect. The process can be stimulated by touching the leaves.

A Bolton's Bench was built around a cluster of yew trees on top of a high mound which may date back to the Iron Age. It was named after Lord Bolton, who was Lord Warden of the Forest in 1688, and the site commands good views over the surrounding countryside.

B Matley is a very attractive wood containing a variety of unusual trees, including several species of oak.

It has not always been so peaceful for, during World War 1, the area to the north-west of the wood was the site of Matley Trench Mortar School. This was closed in 1918 to be replaced by a War Dog Training School, training dogs to carry messages during battle. Up to 200 animals were kept here but there were complaints when the dogs injured and killed some of the commoners' animals. Consequently, the school was closed down in 1919.

Over

6 *Cross the bridge and head south, joining a distinct path in the wetland area. Follow this until it rejoins The Ridge, then turn right back to Bolton's Bench.*

5 *Turn left on to a broad grassy track which skirts the edge of Longwater Lawn and eventually meets the river at a footbridge.*

4 *Turn left and follow the track across the infant Beaulieu River, and go straight on until it approaches the woodland surrounding Ashurst Lodge (watch for rhododendrons!).*

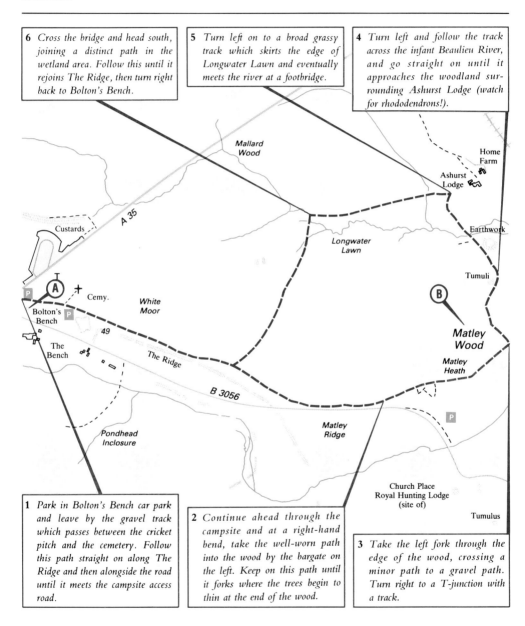

1 *Park in Bolton's Bench car park and leave by the gravel track which passes between the cricket pitch and the cemetery. Follow this path straight on along The Ridge and then alongside the road until it meets the campsite access road.*

2 *Continue ahead through the campsite and at a right-hand bend, take the well-worn path into the wood by the bargate on the left. Keep on this path until it forks where the trees begin to thin at the end of the wood.*

3 *Take the left fork through the edge of the wood, crossing a minor path to a gravel path. Turn right to a T-junction with a track.*

HAMPTON RIDGE AND LATCHMORE BROOK

5½ miles (9 km) Moderate

Latchmore Bottom used to be crossed by old fern tracks, made by the carts of commoners who had loaded them with bracken. This would be cut from the end of August and had a wide variety of uses, such as animal bedding or covering clamps of potatoes. Only a small amount is cut today, mainly as bedding for ponies.

The countryside in this part of the Forest is formed of more-or-less parallel valleys separated by gravel-topped ridges. Latchmore Brook flows down one of these valley bottoms, flanked on the one side by Hampton Ridge and by Hasley Hill on the other.

Latchmore Bottom is a singularly peaceful place. The brook winds its way progressively through marsh and grassy lawn and, in the summertime, often the only witnesses are the multicoloured herds of ponies and cattle that assemble here in peaceful cohabitation. For this place is one of the Forest 'shades' – more exposed, breezy sites that attract the animals in the summer when they wish to keep cool. Latchmore Bottom is an unusual site for a shade because they usually occur on high ground, but the bottom is open, spacious, and close to water. The ponies may be seen standing head to tail, intermittently whisking the flies from their partners.

A There are fine views over the Forest from this elevated ground. They have been admired though for many centuries for Hampton Ridge was an ancient trade route for the export of pottery to the Avon valley and beyond. The clay was excavated locally and the pottery made during Roman times at many sites in the Forest, including nearby Sloden and Islands Thorns. As well as meeting local demand, the potters supplied Roman army posts throughout the country. This century, the ridge was used for less peaceful purposes when 5000 acres (2000 ha) in the area were assigned as a bombing range just after the beginning of World War 2. Bomb craters can still be seen, some filled with water to form strikingly circular ponds.

Over

1 *From Ogdens car park cross the brook by the footbridge and continue uphill along the gravel track. Pass through the car park at the top and where the track meets the road turn right down the main track. A short walk to the left just past the triangulation point gives good views to the north and west as well.*

2 *Take the left-hand fork and, at the next junction, take the right-hand path. Continue on this path over a crossing track to a junction in front of a small copse on the left.*

3 *Turn right and follow the track into the wood. Go ahead at the junction and bear right uphill to where a grassy path crosses the track.*

4 *Turn left, cross the brook, and go through the gate on to the ride. Turn right for 300 yards (275 m) to where a gravel track crosses the ride.*

Tumulus

Alderhill Bottom

Amberwood Inclosure

A Hampton Ridge

100

103

Tumulus

Tumulus

Alderhill Inclosure

Sloden Inclosure

Windmill Hill

Windmillhill Pond

Abbots Well

Latchmore Brook

Ogdens Farm

Watergreen Bottom

Earthwork

Hasley Hill

6 *Turn right down the red sandy path and, where it splits, take the right-hand fork down to Latchmore Brook. Turn left on to a faint path just before the brook and return to the car park.*

Hasley Inclosure

5 *Turn left through the gate and continue to a T-junction with a gravel track. Turn right and stay on this track, leaving the wood and crossing the heath to a junction just before the gate and fence of Hasley Inclosure.*

49

EYEWORTH AND BRAMSHAW TELEGRAPH

5½ miles (9 km) Strenuous; some rough, wet ground, a compass is useful

A beautiful pond, a windswept heath, and a quiet wooded valley are the main ingredients of this interesting walk. It begins from the sheltered, tree-fringed edge of Eyeworth pond, a home for many waterfowl including several species of duck.

Nearby, the seeping waters of a chalybeate spring have turned the ground bright orange. The water was once known for its healing powers, especially for sore eyes and skin disorders.

Past the pond, the route climbs rough, boggy heath on to one of the gravel-capped ridges characteristic of the northern forest. From here, there are views of the Hampshire chalklands strung along the north-western horizon while, to the south, banks of trees and acres of clearings provide inviting views into Islands Thorns Inclosure. Be warned, though, that the northerly winds are as unobstructed as the views, so do not be caught without windproofs on a cold day!

A In the latter part of the last century, Eyeworth Lodge and its surrounding land were leased from the Crown by the Schultz gunpowder company, who chose the site for its seclusion and the abundance of local charcoal – a vital ingredient in the manufacture of gunpowder.

The nearby tributary to Latchmore Brook was dammed to form what we now know as Eyeworth pond – its water was used in the manufacturing process and to power machinery. Unfortunately, much to the annoyance of the commoners, the stream was also used as a drain for toxic waste which made the water from Latchmore Brook undrinkable to their stock.

The manager lived in the Lodge and some of the employees in wooden huts, while others came in from as far away as Fordingbridge, attracted by good 'danger money'. The actual factory consisted of wooden huts, dispersed to minimize the risk of a chain reaction if an explosion occurred in one of them. The finished product was stored in brick and earth bunkers before being taken out by horse-drawn wagons along the specially constructed track past the road. The invention of dynamite and other explosives made the factory redundant early this century.

B The curious name of Bramshaw Telegraph, given to a spot on high ground at the Forest's north-east edge, is all that remains of what was once part of a 'state of the art' communications system.

During the first half of the nineteenth century, messages between London, Portsmouth, and Plymouth were passed along lines of semaphore signalling stations positioned on high ground. Each station was usually manned by three men, one constantly watching nearby stations for signals. Messages were passed using a range of sixty-seven signals representing phrases, words, and numbers. It is reputed that the Greenwich Mean Time signal – so important for nautical navigation – could be passed from London to Plymouth in forty-five seconds!

Over

0 _____ 1 mile
0 _____ 1 km

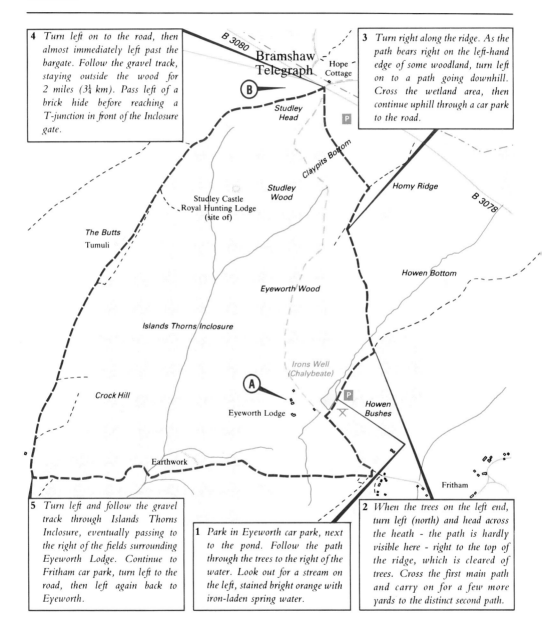

4 *Turn left on to the road, then almost immediately left past the bargate. Follow the gravel track, staying outside the wood for 2 miles (3¼ km). Pass left of a brick hide before reaching a T-junction in front of the Inclosure gate.*

3 *Turn right along the ridge. As the path bears right on the left-hand edge of some woodland, turn left on to a path going downhill. Cross the wetland area, then continue uphill through a car park to the road.*

B 3080

Bramshaw Telegraph

Hope Cottage

B

Studley Head

Claypits Bottom

Studley Wood

Homy Ridge

B 3078

Studley Castle
Royal Hunting Lodge
(site of)

The Butts
Tumuli

Howen Bottom

Eyeworth Wood

Islands Thorns Inclosure

Irons Well
(Chalybeate)

A

Crock Hill

P

Howen Bushes

Eyeworth Lodge

Earthwork

Fritham

5 *Turn left and follow the gravel track through Islands Thorns Inclosure, eventually passing to the right of the fields surrounding Eyeworth Lodge. Continue to Fritham car park, turn left to the road, then left again back to Eyeworth.*

1 *Park in Eyeworth car park, next to the pond. Follow the path through the trees to the right of the water. Look out for a stream on the left, stained bright orange with iron-laden spring water.*

2 *When the trees on the left end, turn left (north) and head across the heath - the path is hardly visible here - right to the top of the ridge, which is cleared of trees. Cross the first main path and carry on for a few more yards to the distinct second path.*

HATCHET POND

2 miles (3¼ km) Easy; boggy in parts

Although at first sight flat and featureless, 4000 years of human activities – from Bronze Age earthworks to twentieth-century runways – lie concealed among the gorse and heather of Beaulieu Heath. This short walk passes some of these relics as it ambles around one of the Forest's most beautiful ponds.

2 *Turn left after passing through the not-too-obvious line of earthworks, and follow the path parallel to them as far as a boggy area.*

1 *Park in Hatchet Pond car park. Head westwards along the water's edge and, after leaving the pond, take the path ahead, angling slightly from the road and passing to the left of a large stand of Scots pines.*

Furzey Lodge

B 3055

Tumulus

Hatchet Pond

Earthwork

Mill

A

Hatchet Moor

East Boldre

B

Beaulieu Heath Airfield

B 3054

3 *Cross the stream to the right of the small pond, then bear left at the junction. Keep bearing left until the path approaches a wet area at the end of Hatchet Pond, and follow the path away from the water. Skirt to the right of a small pond and then follow the path close to its edge as far as a concrete track.*

Bagshot Moor

4 *Turn left along the track towards the parking area and turn right along a path leading from the turning circle at the end. Follow this path alongside Hatchet Pond back to the car park.*

A Hatchet Pond derives its name from a hatch gate that led into the heath from nearby farmland. It was formed from a series of marl pits which were flooded to supply water to a nearby mill. Marl is a mixture of lime and clay and was used to improve farmland. The pond is now a haven for anglers and wildlife.

B Flying started on Beaulieu Heath with a private flying school in 1910, but it was not until 1942 that it developed into an important airfield. It was finally closed in 1960 and largely dismantled, but there are still remains of the runways and gun emplacements.

Walk 24
WILVERLEY INCLOSURE

3¼ miles (5¼ km) Easy

0 _____ 1 mile
0 _____ 1 km

This is a fairly undemanding walk along good tracks among quiet woodland. First of all, though, you pass a grim reminder of the fate of those caught in the act of smuggling or robbery.

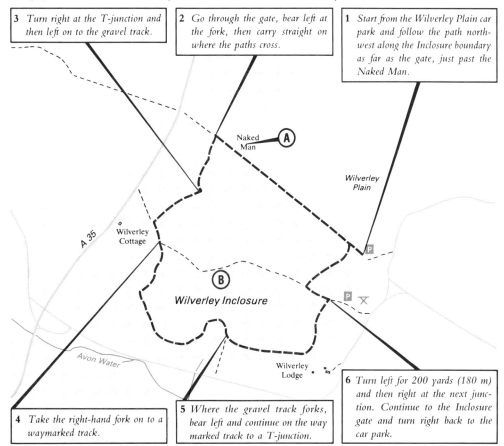

3 *Turn right at the T-junction and then left on to the gravel track.*

2 *Go through the gate, bear left at the fork, then carry straight on where the paths cross.*

1 *Start from the Wilverley Plain car park and follow the path north-west along the Inclosure boundary as far as the gate, just past the Naked Man.*

Naked Man **(A)**

Wilverley Plain

A 35 Wilverley Cottage

(B)

Wilverley Inclosure

Avon Water

Wilverley Lodge

6 *Turn left for 200 yards (180 m) and then right at the next junction. Continue to the Inclosure gate and turn right back to the car park.*

4 *Take the right-hand fork on to a waymarked track.*

5 *Where the gravel track forks, bear left and continue on the waymarked track to a T-junction.*

A This once great oak tree, the Naked Man, was used as a gibbet. It may formerly have resembled the body of a man, or at least it did in 1789 when its present name appears on a map of that date. It now stands only about 10 feet (3 m) high, badly decimated by the ravages of time.

B Wilverley is one of the largest Inclosures in the Forest, first inclosed in 1775 and planted largely with oak in 1809. It was re-inclosed in 1895 and, in the following year, many of the oaks were felled after showing poor growth on the gravelly soil. They were replaced with Scots pine and larch and later with Douglas fir. There are fallow and roe deer in the wood and birdwatchers may find nuthatches, treecreepers, several kinds of tits, and green woodpeckers.

53

STUBBS WOOD AND FRAME WOOD

3½ miles (5½ km) Easy; some mud, a compass is useful

This is an ideal walk for the first-time visitor to the New Forest, for these Ancient and Ornamental Woods would probably fit most people's image of the 'real Forest'.

Stubbs and Frame Wood are old, mature woodland and, to enter their confines, is almost like stepping back in time to medieval England and into the wildwood of past centuries. Old oaks, beech, birch, and holly form beautiful open woodland accompanied by the brighter greens of the ferns and mosses. Several watercourses wander through it all – the streams are described locally as 'gutters' but are called 'waters' elsewhere in the Forest.

The tangle of twisted, decaying oaks suddenly gives way to open, sunlit glades that are frequently occupied by grazing animals and, on a lazy summer's day, presents a most peaceful scene. Frame Wood is similar to Stubbs but with fewer glades and, since 1960, has been successfully left to re-generate by itself, despite the intense grazing from ponies and deer.

Frame Heath Inclosure, on the other hand, was first planted in 1852 and contains a large proportion of conifers. This part of the Forest to the east of Brockenhurst and to the south of the Southampton to Bournemouth railway, is favoured by the sika deer. They were introduced into Britain from Japan in 1860 and kept on the Beaulieu estate, from which two pairs were released in 1904 and 1905. There are now approximately 150 in the Forest.

A Furzey Lodge is a contrasting mixture of old cottages and modern houses. The oldest dwellings clearly show the traditional building material of mud walling, or 'dob', which was still being used in the 1920s. It was made from clayey loam to which was added small stones and heather or straw. These were then mixed together – probably by trampling – and applied or 'dobbed' on to stone or brick foundations. It was a slow process because only about 2 feet (60 cm) could be added at any one time and the mud had to dry out thoroughly between applications. This could take between one and two weeks.

Over

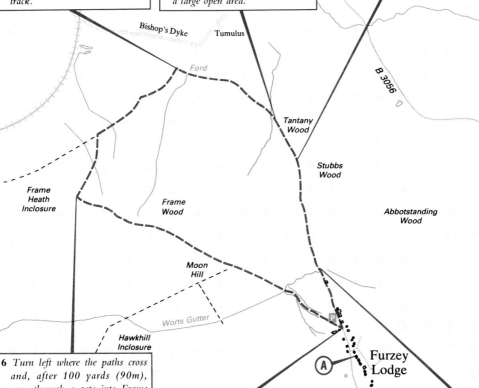

5 *Turn sharp left along the edge of the wood and, after 250 yards (230 m), enter Frame Heath Inclosure through a gate. Follow the gravel track, passing two more gravel tracks off to the left before turning left down a third grassy track.*

4 *Enter the wood in the corner of the clearing - the path is not too well defined at first. Cross a small stream and follow the now distinct path for 1/2 mile (800 m), eventually crossing a ruined concrete ford just before entering a large open area.*

3 *At the clearing, bear slightly left and head north-west along a grassy track, keeping to the left-hand edge of the open area.*

Bishop's Dyke

Tumulus

Ford

B 3056

Tantany Wood

Stubbs Wood

Frame Heath Inclosure

Frame Wood

Abbotstanding Wood

Moon Hill

Worts Gutter

Hawkhill Inclosure

A

Furzey Lodge

6 *Turn left where the paths cross and, after 100 yards (90m), pass through a gate into Frame Wood. Carry straight on, eventually passing through a gate into Hawkshill Inclosure where the path joins a gravel track and continues on across heathland back to the car park.*

1 *From Rans Wood car park in Furzey Lodge, go back to the road and turn left. Continue past the houses and eventually pass to the left of a white house.*

2 *Cross the bridge over Worts Gutter and carry on for ½ mile (800 m) northwards along a broad path through Stubbs Wood to a clearing.*

THE PORTUGUESE FIREPLACE AND ACRES DOWN

3½ miles (5½ km) Moderate. Compass Useful

The sight of an isolated stone fireplace standing alone in a piece of open Forest can come as a surprise. But there it is at the beginning of the walk, a reminder of the Forest's contribution during World War 1.

After World War 2, Acres Down was littered with live explosives, but today, walkers can ramble safely along the heath and enjoy the wide views from the open hilltop over the undulating Forest scenery and south as far as the Isle of Wight.

The trees on this walk are a mixture of conifers and deciduous. Among the latter are sweet chestnut, birch, oak, holly, pollarded beech, and the occasional alder buckthorn and rowan. In several places, there are instances of oak growing among holly where the holly has protected the vulnerable oak saplings. A lucky and keen-eyed visitor may also spot a roe deer, in decline since the early 1970s, and now numbering only around 250.

A The three-tiered stone hearth has recently been restored and marks the site of a Portuguese army camp during World War 1. There were once numerous buildings and tramlines, and the concrete foundations are still in existence. The soldiers worked as lumberjacks, helping to produce timber for the war effort, and the fireplace – originating from the cookhouse – was preserved in memory to the soldiers who camped here.

Over

3 *Continue ahead through the gate, gradually bearing right over Bagshot Gutter into open woodland and eventually meeting a gravel track. Continue on this past Acres Down car park to a junction of tracks before a house.*

4 *Turn right uphill and where the track bears left take the track on the right leading to a wooden barrier. Where the track splits take the right fork and continue for approx ¼ mile to the next fork.*

5 *Be careful to take the left fork heading south east and continue downhill into the wood. Cross the stream to a junction with a grassy track that angles back to the right.*

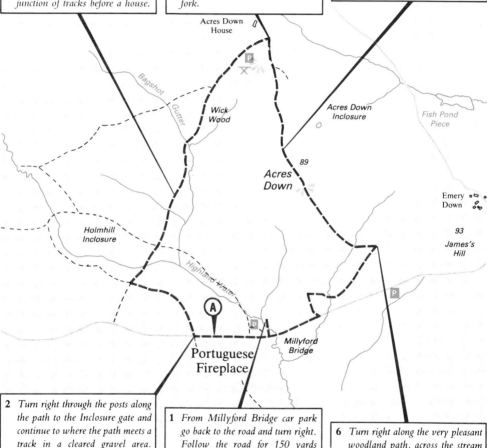

2 *Turn right through the posts along the path to the Inclosure gate and continue to where the path meets a track in a cleared gravel area. Turn right, cross Highland Water, and continue straight on over the crossing track to another gate.*

1 *From Millyford Bridge car park go back to the road and turn right. Follow the road for 150 yards (135 m) past the Portuguese Fireplace to the wooden posts on the right.*

6 *Turn right along the very pleasant woodland path, across the stream once again to a clearing. Turn left to the road and then right back to the car park.*

PICKET POST AND RIDLEY WOOD

4 miles (6½ km) Moderate

The fairly wild, open nature of the heath around Picket Post is characteristic of the place, for it had a reputation as a refuge for smugglers, poachers, and outcasts.

Ridley Wood, too, had its connections with smuggling. Just to the south-west lies Smuggler's Way, part of a route into the Forest from the Avon Valley, and the sunken way at the western edge of Ridley Wood is reputed to have been a continuation of the path. It also probably served as a market place, with buyers coming from all over the south and west of England to purchase fine wares, such as lace and embroideries, that had come from around the world.

Less imagination is needed perhaps to appreciate the beautiful old pollarded beeches and oaks in this, one of the oldest woods in the Forest. Looking at the huge trunks and twisted branches, one is certainly given an impression of age and, fortunately, documentary evidence has survived that gives clues to their possible date. In 1565, for instance, Roger Taverner – the Queen's Surveyor – referred in his *Book of Survey of Royal Forests* to 20 acres (8 ha) of oaks that had been topped and, in 1571, it is recorded that one tenant had pollarded 200 trees in the wood. If they were already old enough to be described as trees, they would have been planted decades earlier, making them very old indeed.

A The view from Picket Post is extensive but the noisy intrusion of the road shatters the peace. There used to be a pub here, illegally built in the Forest, but it became an unruly establishment and was closed down and converted into a tea shop. This has since disappeared under the tarmac of the A31.

The name of the place has uncertain origins. One theory connects it with the picket of soldiers billeted here to cope with the local smugglers. However, this spelling does not appear on maps of that time. Rather it was spelt 'picked', an old word meaning pointed and which is present elsewhere in the Forest. In this instance, it probably referred to the angle of the roads that met here, where a post stood nearby.

Over

0   1 mile

0   1 km

2 At the junction about 100 yards (90 m) from the A31, turn right for ¼ mile (400 m) to a crossing track. Turn left, cross Mill Lawn Brook, and over the first crossing path to the next crossing of tracks just past the wood on the right.

3 Turn right and continue straight ahead over the heath at the crossing track, eventually passing through a pleasant pine copse and over two footbridges uphill to a junction with a well-worn path.

4 Turn right for ⅓ mile to a junction with a minor path just before a lone pine tree. Fork right and follow the path as it peels of downhill to the right as far as a footbridge.

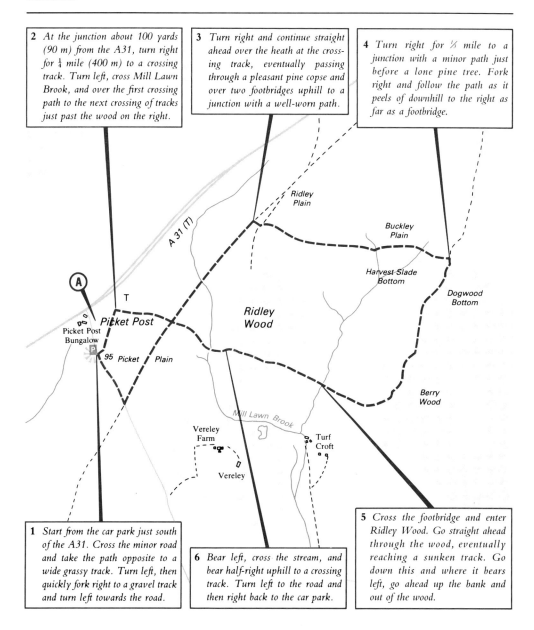

Ridley Plain

A 31 (T)

Buckley Plain

Harvest Slade Bottom

Dogwood Bottom

(A)

T

Picket Post

Picket Post Bungalow

Ridley Wood

95 Picket Plain

Berry Wood

Mill Lawn Brook

Vereley Farm

Turf Croft

Vereley

1 Start from the car park just south of the A31. Cross the minor road and take the path opposite to a wide grassy track. Turn left, then quickly fork right to a gravel track and turn left towards the road.

6 Bear left, cross the stream, and bear half-right uphill to a crossing track. Turn left to the road and then right back to the car park.

5 Cross the footbridge and enter Ridley Wood. Go straight ahead through the wood, eventually reaching a sunken track. Go down this and where it bears left, go ahead up the bank and out of the wood.

Walk 28

OBER HEATH AND QUEEN BOWER

3½ miles (5½ km) Easy

All the major elements of the New Forest are contained in this short walk – heathland, woodland, stream, and lawn. The presence of grazing animals seems to make the scenery complete.

Initially though, the landscape may seem less than natural, for Whitefield Moor, lying just to the west, is an expanse of improved pasture. During World War 2, this site was part of several thousand acres ploughed up to grow crops under the New Forest Pastoral Development Scheme. Once the national emergency was over, the moor was ploughed once again and, in 1948, sown with clover and grasses. It now provides pasture superior to that of the natural Forest Lawn.

A Queen Bower is a renowned beauty spot, and understandably so, for the place has a peaceful, contemplative atmosphere. The stream glides by lovely old oaks set in lush Forest lawn and, in summer, is graced by several varieties of butterflies.

The Bower is said to have been the favourite walk of one of our medieval queens. There is some confusion as to which one – Eleanor, wife of Edward I or Philippa, wife of Edward III. Whichever it may be, the royal patronage is traditionally held to have given this place its name.

Over

0   1 mile

0   1 km

4 *Bear right after crossing the bridge and follow the path through the bushes, eventually entering Poundhill Heath. Take the right hand fork, follow the path parallel with the Inclosure boundary and go straight on into the wood ahead.*

5 *Turn right in front of the stream, cross the bridge, continue ahead and follow the path between the boundary fence and the river. Continue on to a gravel track.*

6 *Turn right and cross the bridge. Follow the gravel track, which later becomes a tarmac road, back to the car park.*

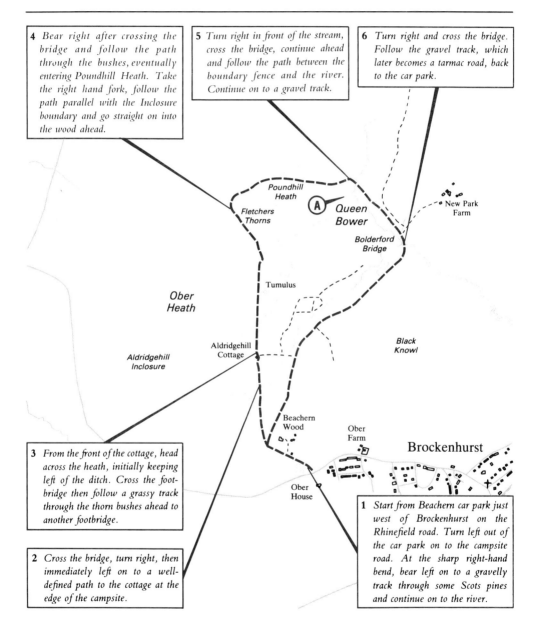

3 *From the front of the cottage, head across the heath, initially keeping left of the ditch. Cross the footbridge then follow a grassy track through the thorn bushes ahead to another footbridge.*

2 *Cross the bridge, turn right, then immediately left on to a well-defined path to the cottage at the edge of the campsite.*

1 *Start from Beachern car park just west of Brockenhurst on the Rhinefield road. Turn left out of the car park on to the campsite road. At the sharp right-hand bend, bear left on to a gravelly track through some Scots pines and continue on to the river.*

61

KNIGHTWOOD OAK AND HOLIDAYS HILL

3¼ miles (5¼ km) Easy

This is a fine woodland walk, passing through the oaks and conifers of Holidays Hill, one of the Forest's oldest Inclosures dating from 1676. Brinken Wood has an even more ancient feel, with Highland Water wandering lazily through holly and contorted oaks while, nearby, there are sunny glades edged with frosted silver birch. The route also touches on the Forestry Commission's Tall Trees Walk, alongside Rhinefield Ornamental Drive, where conifer specimens from around the world were planted during the middle of the last century and have now reached impressive proportions.

A Knightwood Oak, the most famous tree of the Forest, is at least 350 years old and probably much older. It owes its great age to the practice of pollarding (from the French *poil* – to behead): the limbs of trees were cut off leaving a permanent trunk or 'bolling', about 10 feet (3 m) high, from which new shoots would quickly sprout. These would be harvested periodically to provide winter fodder for animals, fuel and wood for fences and so on. This process can go on almost indefinitely without the tree becoming exhausted.

Because of the scarcity of full-grown trees to provide timber for shipbuilding, pollarding was made illegal in 1698. The Knightwood Oak and the many other oaks and beeches throughout the forest that show the characteristic pollarded crown could, therefore, have been in existence for some considerable time before this date.

The trunk of the Knightwood Oak has a massive 23-foot (7 m) girth 4 feet (1¼ m) above the ground. Sadly, it is now past its best and losing some of its great limbs but it still stands about 100 feet (30 m) high.

B Reptiles are shy, often well-camouflaged creatures rarely seen except by the most sharp-eyed walker, so the Reptiliary provides a good opportunity to see something of these elusive Forest inhabitants. It was set up by the Forestry Commission to educate the public and to breed rarer species for the wild. The reptiles live in open concrete pens, landscaped to produce their favourite environments. The visitor can see the large olive green grass snake, the venomous adder with its zig-zag markings, and the rare, silvery smooth snake, along with lizards and toads.

Over

2 *Turn right along the gravel track. Go ahead where the paths cross, and then turn right at the second crossing point where a gravel track comes in from the left.*

3 *Turn right on to the main gravel track, through the Reptiliary and the Holidays Hill campsite to the A35.*

4 *Cross the road and go over the fence opposite, then follow a grassy path ahead through the wood as far as a footbridge. Do not cross this but bear right (south-west) across a grassy lawn until a path is reached. Cross the open glade to a small footbridge.*

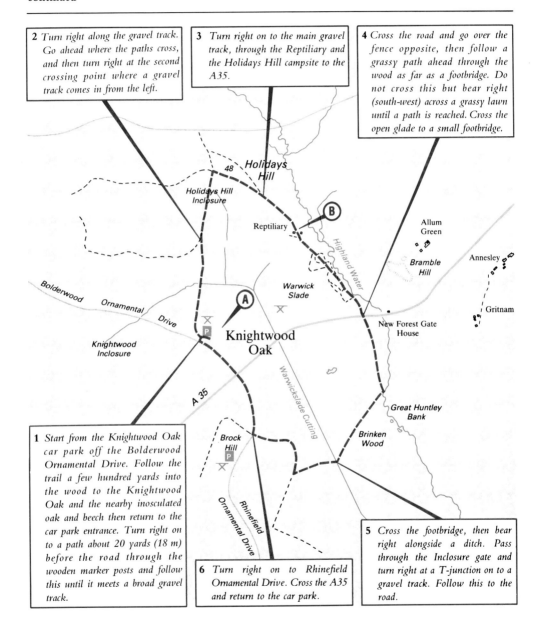

1 *Start from the Knightwood Oak car park off the Bolderwood Ornamental Drive. Follow the trail a few hundred yards into the wood to the Knightwood Oak and the nearby inosculated oak and beech then return to the car park entrance. Turn right on to a path about 20 yards (18 m) before the road through the wooden marker posts and follow this until it meets a broad gravel track.*

5 *Cross the footbridge, then bear right alongside a ditch. Pass through the Inclosure gate and turn right at a T-junction on to a gravel track. Follow this to the road.*

6 *Turn right on to Rhinefield Ornamental Drive. Cross the A35 and return to the car park.*

Walk 30

RHINEFIELD ORNAMENTAL DRIVE

2¾ miles (4½ km) Easy

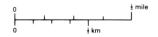

This walk combines the three trails laid out by the Forestry Commission in the vicinity of Rhinefield Ornamental Drive. They are a popular feature of the Forest and it is hard to believe that, until 1938, the road was a woodland track. The trees beside the drive were originally planted in 1859 and four of them are the largest of their species in Britain.

---

1 *Start from Brock Hill car park off the Rhinefield Ornamental Drive about ½ mile (800 m) south of the A35. Turn left out of the car park on to the road then turn sharp left just before the A35 on to a grassy track. Continue to a junction with a gravel track.*

2 *Go straight on over the gravel track and on up to Brock Hill, then bear half right ahead onto the waymarked path. Follow the path to a junction with a gravel path and turn left to another T-junction.*

3 *Turn right just before the road on to a path with red waymarks. Follow this parallel to the road for 2/3 mile (1 km), crossing the footbridge to a junction with a gravel track. Turn right then immediately left and continue to a bridge, following the yellow markers.*

4 *Cross the Black Water and continue alongside before shortly recrossing it. Follow the yellow waymarked path through the arboretum to the road.*

5 *Cross the road and turn left in the car park. Follow the red waymarked path parallel with the road back to Brock Hill car park.*

T · Brock Hill · A · Brinken Wood · Vinney Ridge Inclosure · B · C · D · Poundhill Inclosure · A 35 · Rhinefield Ornamental Drive

---

A The unusual knoll of Brock Hill is the site of an old badger sett. The animal's Saxon name of 'broc' is found elsewhere in the Forest, such as at nearby Brockenhurst.

B The tallest of these superb, pyramidal Wellingtonia trees is 165 feet (50 m) tall but even then is only half the height it would reach in its native California.

C The Arboretum was originally a wood of oak and Douglas fir which was cleared and planted with trees in 1960.

D Rhinefield was first inclosed in 1700 and this section of ditch and bank represents part of the first Inclosure boundary. Construction was obviously very hard work – the ditch is 5 feet (1½ m) deep and the 6-foot (1¾ m) high bank is topped by oak palings.

64